Ribbon Flowers
Paper Flowers

Ribbon Flowers Paper Flowers

YURI UCHIYAMA

photographs by Akira Tsukui

Published by Kodansha International Ltd.
Tokyo, New York and San Francisco

ACKNOWLEDGMENTS

The author and photographer wish to thank the Daimaru Department Store and the Ginza Matsuzakaya Department Store for the loan of the vases and dolls used in the color plates and also Nobu Maeda for her valuable help in the translation of the manuscript.

DISTRIBUTORS:
UNITED STATES: Harper & Row, Publishers, Inc.
10 East 53rd Street, New York, New York 10022
CANADA: Fitzhenry & Whiteside Limited
150 Lesmill Road, Don Mills, Ontario
CENTRAL AND SOUTH AMERICA: Feffer & Simons Inc.
31 Union Square, New York, New York 10003
BRITISH COMMONWEALTH (excluding Canada and the Far East): TABS,
51 Weymouth Street, London WIN 3LE
EUROPE: Boxerbooks Inc.
Limmatstrasse 111, 8031 Zurich
THAILAND: Central Department Store Ltd.
306 Silom Road, Bangkok
HONG KONG: Books for Asia Ltd.
379 Prince Edward Road, Kowloon
THE FAR EAST: Japan Publications Trading Company
P.O. Box 5030, Tokyo International, Tokyo

Published by Kodansha International Ltd., 2–12–21 Otowa, Bunkyo-ku, Tokyo 112 and Kodansha International/USA, Ltd., 10 East 53rd Street, New York, New York 10022 and 44 Montgomery Street, San Francisco, California 94104.
Copyright © 1974 by Kodansha International Ltd.

LCC 73-89697
ISBN 0-87011-221-x
JBC 5076-784328-2361

First edition, 1974

CONTENTS

PREFACE

Whenever I see a beautiful flower I feel an overwhelming and instinctive desire to preserve it forever, a natural and human reaction to the exquisite things of this world. But flowers are living things too—they bloom and then wither away, a constant reminder of the transience of life itself. Yet it is this mysterious beauty of flowers, which grow from tiny buds into magnificent blossoms, that has also inspired me to observe Nature much more closely and even to imitate it.

To try and reproduce Nature as perfectly as possible is what I shall call the realistic approach to flower-making. It is also possible, as well as rewarding, to conjure up and create a flower from one's imagination alone, and thus to bring about fantastic, wild and gorgeous examples which can be used to lend a unique touch to any room, be it a bedroom, a shop window or even a public gallery.

The materials I have used to make my bouquets are the simplest—just crepe paper, ribbon and scraps of fabric. Most of you will already be familiar with paper flowers, but ribbon flowers is an art that is only found in Japan. I still remember my first attempt with ribbon, some 18 years ago, when I made a simple white lily to decorate my bedroom. But ribbons today come in such a rich variety of colors and textures that it is possible to create any flower you wish, whether it is one that blooms in your backyard or one that you have only seen in photographs.

The flowers in this book are some of the ribbon, paper and fabric flowers that I have made myself and I can only hope that they will guide you well as you make your own beautiful creations. I am certain that they will give you as many pleasurable hours as they have given me.

Yuri Uchiyama

Tokyo,
April 1974

MATERIALS AND BASIC STEPS

CREPE PAPER: There are two kinds of crepe paper, single and double crepe. Double crepe is thicker than single crepe and has a front surface which is distinguishable from the back, an important detail to remember when using crepe to make flowers. All the flowers in this book, including the ribbon flowers, can be made with crepe paper.

RIBBONS: The ribbons used in this book are made from rayon, acetate and other synthetic materials which have unfrayable edges and are intended for flower-making. These synthetic ribbons come in several widths, from 1/2 in. to 3 in., and they are available in most handicraft stores in a variety of types. The choice includes *acetate ribbon*, a hard, glossy, synthetic ribbon; *ombre*, an acetate ribbon dyed in gradation; *silk ribbon*, thin and rather like taffeta; *silk ombre*, a synthetic silk ribbon dyed in gradation; *rayon satin ribbon*, with a shiny finish; *velvet ribbon*; *velvelour art ribbon*, a velvet ribbon dyed in gradation; *velita*, a ribbon resembling velveteen; and *glitter ribbon*, a sparkling variety used for decoration and gift packaging.

As mentioned earlier, all these ribbons have an unfrayable finish and are therefore hard to the touch. If ordinary ribbon or fabric is used instead, it is best to apply starch to the back of the material first to prevent it from fraying.

WIRES: Special wires for flower-making are sold, cut in lengths of 18 in. (unless otherwise indicated in the text, the length of the wires used is generally 18 in.). It goes without saying that ordinary wire cut in the appropriate lengths can also be substituted, but the special wires for flower-making are sold in different gauges, ranging from #18 to #30 (the higher the number, the thinner the wire).

The thinner wire (#30) is used for making flower and leaf stalks or for attaching flowers and leaves onto the main stem, although several wires gathered together can also be used to make thicker stems.

In Japan, wires wrapped with white, green or brown tape for the backs of petals and leaves can be bought, but when not available, floral tape wound around a piece of thin wire is a good alternative. Wires coated with green paint or bound with green or white or brown paper are also good substitutes.

FLORAL TAPE: This tape is indispensable for giving the finishing touches to stems and calyxes and for preventing the wires and

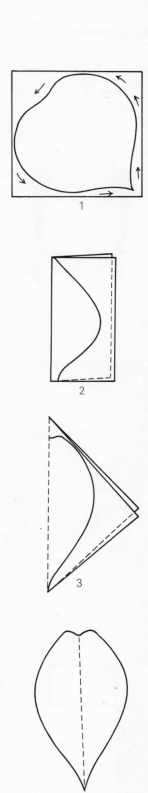

1

2

3

4

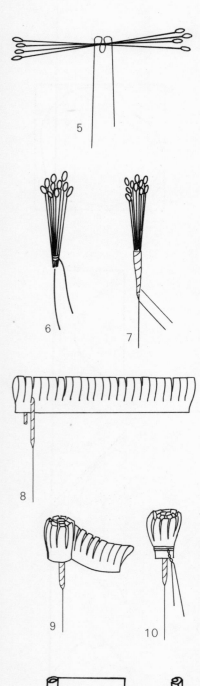

paper from slipping or becoming unmanageable during the process of making the flowers. The tape is sold in most flower shops and comes in half-inch-wide rolls. It is made from a crepelike material with adhesive on the back and so should be stretched when used.

READY-MADE STAMENS: These are sold in various sizes and colors in packages of 72 and with heads at both ends so that they must be bent double when used. If these stamens are not available, the substitutes shown on page 11 will serve just as well (with the exception of some very special types of flowers).

All the tools and materials mentioned above are sold in Japan in handicraft supply shops or in the handicraft sections of department stores. In the United States, floral tape is available at all florists, and more specific information about the materials can be obtained from the following wholesale stores:

Fantasy Store (Howelco Ltd.)
819 Keeaumoku Street
Honolulu, Hawaii 96814

Moskatel (Inarco Corp.)
717-733 S. San Julian Street
Los Angeles, California 290014

BASIC STEPS

HOW TO USE THE PATTERNS: Actual-size patterns are given at the back of the book on pages 126–160. First trace the outline of the petal or leaf, cut it out and place it over the back of the ribbon or crepe paper and draw the shape with a pencil.

HOW TO CUT THE MATERIAL: Before cutting the crepe paper or the ribbon, it is important to notice the direction of the grain, otherwise wavy and convex effects will be difficult to produce. It is advisable to follow closely the arrows marked in the pattern and to arrange the ribbon, fabric or crepe to run in the same direction. After you have drawn the shape of the petal or leaf on the back of the material or paper, cut it out by turning the paper or material as you go along, rather than the scissors, to prevent any angular shapes (figure 1). When complete symmetry is required, first fold the fabric or paper in half, following the indications of the arrows, then cut out the shape (figure 2).

In making symmetrical petals from ribbon, first cut out a square from the strip of ribbon, then fold it diagonally and cut out the shape (figures 3 and 4). This makes it easier to produce convex effects on the petals.

HOW TO MAKE STAMENS:

1. *Using ready-made stamens*: Take the required number of stamens, wind wire around the center, bend them in half and bind them again about 1/6 in. from the base with the wire. Then cover 1 in. of the base with floral tape (figures 5, 6 and 7).

2. *Using a rolled strip*: Cut out a narrow, long strip from the ribbon or crepe paper and make tiny slits about 1/8 in. wide along one edge of the strip. Then take a piece of wire, wind floral tape around its tip, bend the tip into the shape of a horseshoe and hook it in the second slit from one end of the strip. Roll up the strip tightly around the wire from the same end that the wire was hooked in and bind the base with wire, covering about 1 in. of the base with floral tape (figures 8, 9 and 10). This type of stamen is used for poppies and anemones.

3. *Using wire and tape*: Cover a thin piece of wire with floral tape and wind another piece of tape over the tip of the wire (figures 11 and 12). If ribbon strips are used instead of floral tape, apply glue to the back of the strip. This method can be used as a substitute for the ready-made stamens.

HOW TO CREATE CONVEX AND WAVY EFFECTS: Convex shapes can be made with crepe paper by stretching it sideways (figure 13). Ribbon, however, is stretched by applying more force. The wavy effects or the flutes on the edges of the petals are produced by holding the edges tightly with the tips of thumb and forefinger of both hands and then pulling the piece in opposite directions at the same time (figure 14).

In order to curl the tips of petals or leaves backward, press firmly with the blunt end of scissors as shown in figure 15.

HOW TO BIND WITH WIRE: To bind a single petal or leaf with wire, first make small gathers at the base of the petal or leaf and, winding one end of the wire around the base two or three times, tighten it by pulling strongly (figures 16 and 17).

When making flowers which have a great many petals, like dahlias, it is best to link the petals first with wire. This is done by winding wire around the base of one petal as mentioned above, then taking another petal and binding it in the same way until all the petals are linked together (figures 18, 19 and 20). The space between each petal depends on the relationship between the number of petals and the circumference of the central disk of the flower which it encloses.

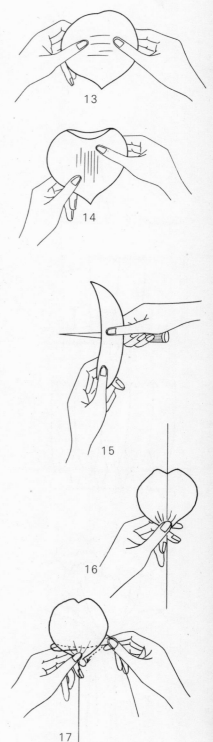

When petals or leaves are to be attached together or to the main stem, twist the wire three or four times around the base about 1/2 in. from the bottom end and then tighten the wire by twisting the two ends around each other two or three times. After using wire, always make sure you cover it with tape in order to give it a neat finish (figure 21).

HOW TO STICK WIRE ON LEAVES OR PETALS: In order to stick taped wire to the back of petals or leaves, place the wire about 1/2 in. or 1 in. from the tip of the leaf or petal down to the base and extend the lower end about 2–3 in. beyond the base of the leaf or petal (figure 22).

When wire is to be attached between two pieces of crepe paper or ribbon, cut out a rectangular or square shape first, place the wire about 1/2 in. from the tip down the center of the back surface of the material or paper and cover the entire back with double-faced tape. Then stick the back of the other piece of material over it and cut out the shape of the petal or leaf (figure 23). Glue or paste may be used instead of double-faced tape.

HOW TO WIND FLORAL TAPE: Stick one end of the tape to the wire and, with the wire and tape that has just been stuck on in the left hand, stretch the floral tape with your right hand and wind it spirally down by rotating the wire (figure 24). Keep the tape taut while winding it down and allow the edges of each coil to overlap very slightly to give the stem or stalk a uniform appearance.

Should you want to make a stem appear thicker, take several pieces of wire and cover them with tape. Next wind tissue paper strips, 1/2 in. or 1 in. wide, over them and cover them once more with tape until the stem is thick enough (figure 25).

When working with very thin wire, a neater finish can be obtained by cutting the width of the tape in half, i.e. making it 1/4 in. wide and then winding it around the wire.

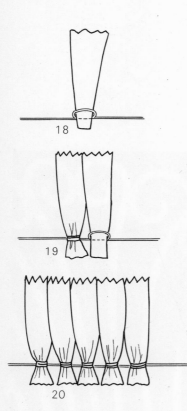

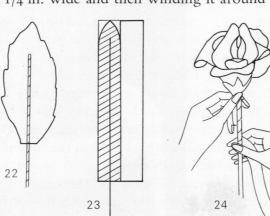

THE FLOWERS

Tulip: *crepe*
Page 49

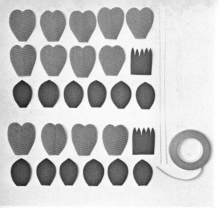

HOW TO MAKE A ROSE

1. The materials necessary for 2 flowers, 2 stems,
   12 leaves and 2 calyxes.

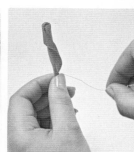

2. Stretch the petal to give it a concave effect.

3. Curl the edges of the petal with the blunt side of a pair
   of scissors.

4. To make the core of the rose, roll up the petal from one
   end and bind the base with wire.

6. To link petals, first bind the base of each petal with wire.

7. Bind the next petal close to the first one with the same
   piece of wire.

5. Cover the base of the
   rolled core with floral
   tape.

8. Wrap the 3 linked petals
   around the core of the rose.

9. Bind the base with wire and
   floral tape.

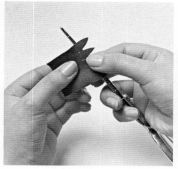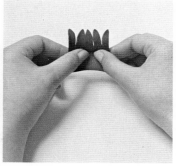

10. When the 5 linked petals have been wrapped around the other 3, attach a piece of stem wire to the base of the rose and bind with floral tape.

11. Curl the calyx outward with the blunt edge of a pair of scissors.

12. Stretch the calyx sideways to create a concave effect.

13. Wrap the calyx around the base of the completed flower and bind with wire.

14. Make small gathers at the base of the leaf, bind with wire and cover the wire with floral tape.

15. Combine 3 leaves on a stalk with floral tape.

16. The leaf stalks are attached to the stem with floral tape.

17. The half-opened rose is made with 4 petals and 6 leaves in the same way.

Miniature
    rose: *crepe*
Page 51

Marguerite: *crepe*
Page 50

Stock: *crepe* ▶
Page 52

Hibiscus: *crepe*
Page 54

18

Wood rose: *crepe*
Page 53

Cosmos: *crepe*
Page 58

Carnation: *ribbon*
Page 88

Hyacinth: *ribbon*
Page 87

Lily: *crepe*
Page 56

Foxglove: *crepe*
Page 60

Snapdragon: *crepe* ▶
Page 62

Gladiolus: *crepe*
Page 64

Rhododendron: *crepe*
Page 68

◄Gentian: *crepe*
Page 66

Edelweiss: *crepe*
Page 70

Bouvardia: *crepe*
Page 72

Anemone: *crepe*
Page 74

Cherry blossom: *crepe*
Page 76

30

Forsythia: *crepe*
Page 66

Gardenia: *crepe*
Page 78

Lily of the valley: *crepe*
Page 80

Daisy: *crepe*
Page 71

Cactus dahlia: *crepe* ▶
Page 84

Pompon dahlia: *crepe*
Page 82

Poppy: *crepe*
Page 86

Evening primrose: *ribbon*
Page 90

Daffodil: *ribbon*
Page 89

Rose: *ribbon* ▶
Page 92

Moth orchid: *crepe*
Page 96

Old World orchid: *ribbon*
Page 94

Magnolia: *ribbon* ▶
Page 98

Camellia: *ribbon*
Page 100

Maple: *ribbon*
Page 108

Red bamboo: *ribbon*
Page 108

Nasturtium: *ribbon*
Page 110

Peach blossom: *ribbon*
Page 102

Rape flower: *ribbon*
Page 104

Iris: *ribbon* ▶
Page 106

Polka dot flower: *fabric*
Stitched flower: *fabric*
Chenille flower: *fabric*
Silk flower: *fabric*
Pages 121–23

Eucalyptus fantasy: *ribbon*
Page 109

Folded paper flower:
Page 124

48

TULIP

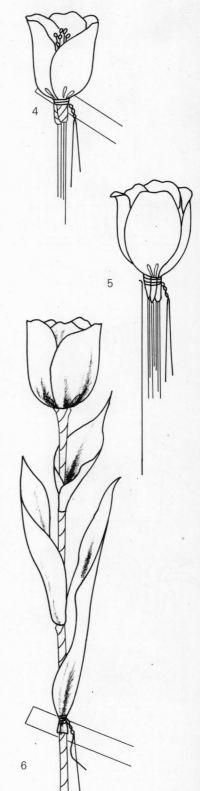

MATERIALS (for 1 stem, 1 flower and 3 leaves)
  PETALS: Red or yellow double crepe paper
  STAMENS: 5 ready-made stamens
  LEAVES: Green double crepe paper
  1 piece of wire (#18), 12 in. long
  11 pieces of wire (#30), 8 in. long
  Green floral tape   Tissue paper   Glue

According to the pattern on page 126, cut out 6 petals from the red or yellow crepe, 2 large leaves and 1 small leaf from the green crepe paper.

Stretch each petal sideways to give it a convex effect, wind a piece of wire (#30) around the base of each and cover it with floral tape, extending the tape 1 in. beyond the base of the petal (figures 1 and 2).

Take 5 stamens, wind floral tape around the center and bend them in half. Bind them together with wire about 1/2 in. from the base and cover with floral tape (figure 3).

Next arrange 3 petals around the stamens (figure 4), bind them with wire (#30) and cover about 1 in. of it with floral tape. Attach the other 3 petals in the same way, making sure that they are placed in an alternating pattern, and bind with floral tape as before (figure 5).

To make the stem, take the long piece of wire (#18), cover it entirely with floral tape and wrap with tissue paper strips cut 1/2 in. wide. Glue down the ends and cover once more with floral tape. About 3 in. from the base of the tulip, cut the tape and attach the small leaf, which should be gathered at the base, to the stem with wire (#30). Repeat the process of covering with tape. Attach the large leaf about 4 in. below the small one, and the remaining leaf about 2 in. below that (figure 6). The leaves should be arranged spirally around the stem and not in a straight line.

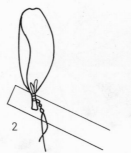

MARGUERITE

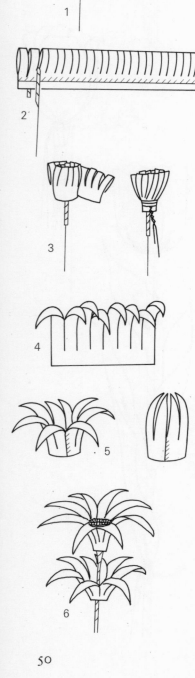

MATERIALS (for 1 flower, 1 bud and 4 leaves)
   PETALS AND BUD: White double crepe paper
   DISK OF FLOWER: Yellow double crepe paper
   LEAVES: Green double crepe paper
   2 pieces of wire (#24), 12 in. long
   4 pieces of wire (#30)
   4 pieces of wire (#26) wrapped with green tape, 5 in. long
   Light green floral tape
   Glue

Working from the pattern on page 126, cut out 3 sets of petals (1 set is for the bud), 2 disks and 4 leaves.

Take a piece of wire (#24), wrap 1 in. of the tip with tape and bend it as shown in figure 1. To make the disk, fold the cut strip in two, with one half 1/8 in. shorter than the other, and glue the two halves together. Cut slits 1/12 in. wide and 1/3 in. long on the folded edge of the strip (figure 2). Hook the wire in the second slit of the disk, roll the strip tightly around the wire and bind the base with wire (#30) and tape (figure 3). Make 2 disks, one for the flower and one for the bud.

The 2 sets of petals for the flower should be curled outward, and 1 set for the bud curled inward (figures 4 and 5). To do this use the blunt edge of a pair of scissors (refer to *Basic Steps*). To make the flower, glue the two ends of the petals together to form a cylindrical shape and place a disk in the center, enclosing this with another set of petals (curled outward) and arranging the petals to form an alternating design (figure 6). Twist wire (#30) around the base and cover 1 in. of it with tape (figure 7).

The bud is made by enclosing the remaining disk with the petals that are curled inward and binding the base with wire (#30) and tape (figure 8).

Next take a piece of wire (#26) and glue it to the back of a leaf. Two leaves are attached below the flower and the bud respectively.

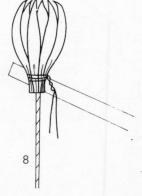

MINIATURE ROSE

MATERIALS (for 1 flower and 3 leaves)
   PETALS: Salmon pink or pink double crepe paper
   LEAVES: Green double crepe paper
   1 piece of wire (#20), 12 in. long
   10 pieces of wire (#30), 8 in. long
   Light green floral tape

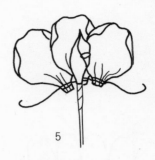

5

Using the pattern on page 127, cut out 11 petals and 3 leaves.

As shown in figure 1, curl the top edges of 10 petals backward, and those of 1 petal forward. Roll up the petal with the edges curled forward and bind the base with wire (#30) and tape, extending it about 1 in. beyond the petal base (figure 2).

Enclose this by rolling 2 petals around it and bind with wire (#30) and tape (figure 3). Then, following figure 4, make a set of 3 petals and another set of 5 petals by linking them together at the base with wire so that their edges overlap slightly (refer to *Materials and Basic Steps* on pages 9–12). Wrap the set of 3 linked petals with the front surface of the paper turned inside, and bind it at the base with wire (#30) and tape. Next wind the 5 linked petals around this and tie in the same way with wire (#30) and tape (figures 5 and 6).

6

The stem wire (#20) is attached to the base of the flower with tape, which is then wound spirally down its entire length.

Take a leaf and bind its base with wire (#30) and tape, extending it 1–2 in. below the base of the leaf (figure 7). Combine 3 leaves as shown in figure 8, attach them to the main stem and wind floral tape down it once more.

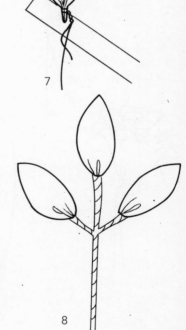

7

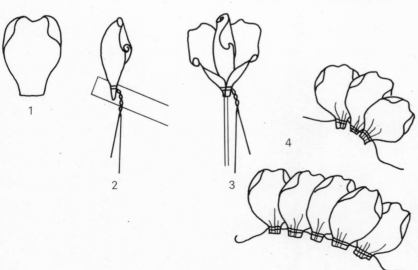

1

2

3

4

8

STOCK

MATERIALS (for 1 stem, 20 flowers, 10 buds, 5 tight buds and
      10 leaves)
  PETALS, BUDS AND LEAVES: Blue or white single crepe paper
3 pieces of wire (#18)
45 pieces of wire (#30), 8 in. long
Blue floral tape

Following the pattern on page 128, cut out 20 sets of petal A
for the flowers, 10 sets of petal B for the buds and 5 sets of petal
C for the tight buds. For the leaves, place two sheets of crepe
paper on top of each other and cut out 5 sets of A and 5 of B.

Make gathers at the base of all the petal strips (A, B and C)
following figure 1 and roll them up from one end. Twist wire
(#30) around the base and bind with tape, extending it 2 in.
beyond the base (figures 2 and 3). When rolling up the petal
A strips, arrange the outer petals to stand a little higher than
the inner ones (figure 4).

The leaf is made with doubled crepe paper and, as shown in
figure 5, it is fixed at the base with wire (#30) and tape.

Using figure 6 as a guide, put 3 pieces of wire (#18) together
for the stem and, beginning from the top, attach the tight buds
made from petal C to the stem with tape at intervals of about
1 in., arranging them in a spiral. Then follow this with the buds
made from petal B and then the flowers from petal A, at
intervals of 1/2 in. The B buds and A flowers have stalks about
1 in. long. Lastly, about 3 in. below the flowers, arrange the
leaves 3 in. apart and attach them to the stem with tape, the A
leaves first and, underneath them, the B leaves.

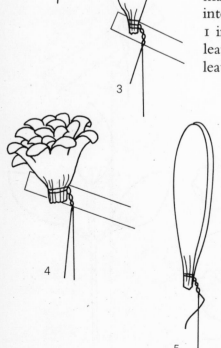

WOOD ROSE

MATERIALS (for 1 bud and 1 flower)
  PETALS AND BUD: Brown or beige double crepe paper
  STAMENS: Beige double crepe paper
  2 pieces of wire (#18)
  15 pieces of wire (#30), 8 in. long
  Brown or beige floral tape   Absorbent cotton

Cut out 6 stamens, 6 small petals (3 for the bud) and 5 large petals according to the pattern on page 127.

Stretch the crepe for the stamens diagonally (figure 1) and place some absorbent cotton 1/2 in. in diameter in the middle. Twist wire (#30) around the neck of the ball. Cover the neck with tape and wind it downward about 1 in. (figure 2).

Hold the petal with both hands and stretch it sideways to make a concave effect on the front of the crepe (figure 3). This process is used for both the large and small petals.

Gather the lower part of the large petal and bind it with wire (#30) 1/2 in. from the bottom. Then cover with tape, extending it about 1 in. (figure 4).

Take 3 stamens, bind them with wire (#30) and wind tape around this (figure 5).

Wrap the stamens with 3 small petals, allowing their edges to overlap (figure 6). Then bind the base with wire (#30) and cover it with tape (figure 7). The bud is completed by attaching the stem wire (#18) to the base and winding tape over it down the length of the stem.

To make the flower, wrap 5 large petals around the 3 small petals of the bud and fix at the base with wire (#30) and tape. Then attach the stem wire (#18) and bind with tape.

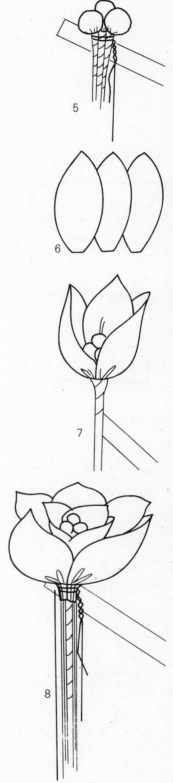

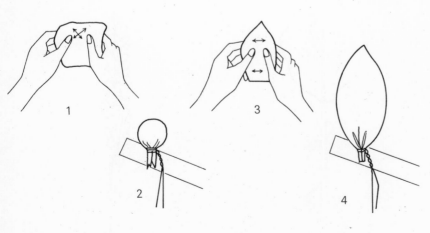

53

HIBISCUS

MATERIALS (for 1 flower and 1 bud)

PETALS AND BUD: Red, white, orange or pink double crepe paper

STAMENS: Yellow double crepe paper

LEAVES: Green double crepe paper

5 pieces of wire (#26) wrapped with white tape, 6 in. long

2 pieces of wire (#22), 10 in. long

10 pieces of wire (#30), 8 in. long

2 pieces of wire (#18)

Green floral tape

Handkerchief   Glue

Working from the pattern on page 129, cut out 8 petals (5 for the flower and 3 for the bud), 6 leaves and 2 stamen strips.

As shown in figure 1, fold each petal in half with the front surface outside. To make creases on the petal, spread out some gauze or a handkerchief, put the folded petal in the center and fold the gauze in two over it diagonally (figure 2). Place your left hand on the petal base and press, and with your right hand grasp one end of the gauze and pull it strongly in the direction of the arrow (figure 3). Now open the petal out and twist inward and outward along the edges to create a wavy effect (figure 4).

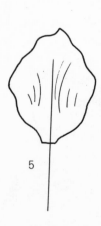

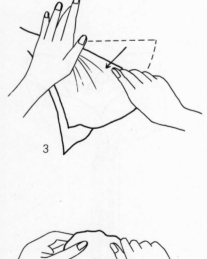

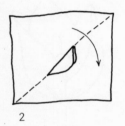

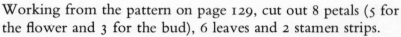

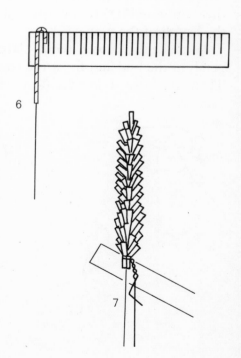

Glue the wire (#26) wrapped with white tape down the back surface of the open petal, 1/2 in. from the tip (figure 5).

To make the stamens, take a piece of wire (#22) and wind tape 4 in. down it. Bend the tip as shown in figure 6 and hook it in the second slit of the stamen strip. Then roll it down with the front surface of the paper outside, so that when complete the stamens will be about 3 in. long (figure 7). Twist wire (#30) around the base and cover about 1 in. of it with tape. Make 2 of the above stamens, one for the flower and one for the bud.

Wrap the stamens with 5 open petals, with the front surface of the paper facing inside, and twist wire around the base. Attach the stem wire (#18) and bind with tape spirally down the rest of the stem (figure 8).

Following figure 9, put the remaining 3 petals in a row with their edges overlapping and the front surface of the crepe facing outward. Place the stamens in the middle of the 3 petals, and after wrapping them around the stamens, twist wire (#30) around the base. Then attach the stem wire (#18) to the base and cover it with tape (figure 10).

The leaf is bound with wire (#30) about 1/2 in. from the base and then wound with tape, extended 1 in. beyond the base (figure 11).

On the stems of both the flower and the bud, attach 3 leaves about 3 in. apart and fix them on with tape (figure 12). The leaf stalks should be about 1/2 in. long.

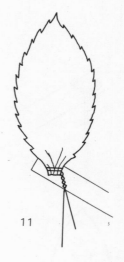

11

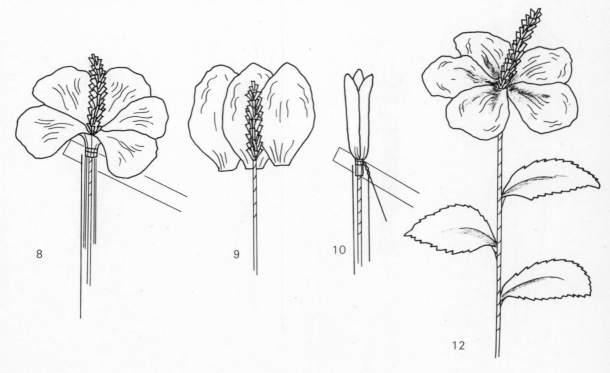

8

9

10

12

LILY

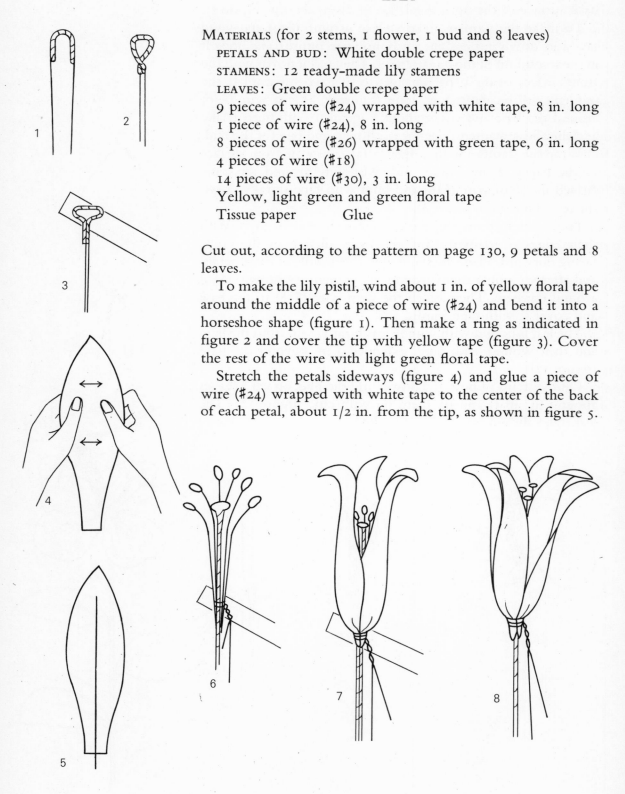

MATERIALS (for 2 stems, 1 flower, 1 bud and 8 leaves)
  PETALS AND BUD: White double crepe paper
  STAMENS: 12 ready-made lily stamens
  LEAVES: Green double crepe paper
  9 pieces of wire (#24) wrapped with white tape, 8 in. long
  1 piece of wire (#24), 8 in. long
  8 pieces of wire (#26) wrapped with green tape, 6 in. long
  4 pieces of wire (#18)
  14 pieces of wire (#30), 3 in. long
  Yellow, light green and green floral tape
  Tissue paper   Glue

Cut out, according to the pattern on page 130, 9 petals and 8 leaves.

To make the lily pistil, wind about 1 in. of yellow floral tape around the middle of a piece of wire (#24) and bend it into a horseshoe shape (figure 1). Then make a ring as indicated in figure 2 and cover the tip with yellow tape (figure 3). Cover the rest of the wire with light green floral tape.

Stretch the petals sideways (figure 4) and glue a piece of wire (#24) wrapped with white tape to the center of the back of each petal, about 1/2 in. from the tip, as shown in figure 5.

Take 6 lily stamens and enclose the pistil, arranging them so that they protrude 1 in. above the pistil (figure 6), and bind them with green tape about 4 in. below the longest stamen. Place 3 petals around the stamens with the front surface of the paper outside and bind the base with wire and tape (figure 7). Arrange 3 more petals around this so that the petals alternate, and bind with wire (#30) as shown in figure 8.

Bind 2 pieces of stem wire (#18) together with green tape and then cover this stem with tissue paper strips 1/2 in. wide, followed by more floral tape (figure 9).

To make the leaves, glue wire (#26) down the center of the back of each leaf 1/2 in. from the tip, and attach one leaf to the stem with wire (#30) about 6 in. below the flower. Cover the wire with tape (figure 10). Add the other leaves to the main stem in a similar manner at intervals of 3–4 in.

Make the bud by wrapping 3 petals around the pistil and stamens in the same way as for the flowers, with the front surface of the paper outside, and bind them together with wire (#30). Attach 2 pieces of stem wire (#18) to the base of the bud with tape, extending it to cover the entire stem. Cover the stem with strips of tissue paper and more tape. The leaves are attached in the same way as above. As a finishing touch, bend the necks of the flower and bud slightly to produce the effect shown in figure 11.

9

10

11

COSMOS

MATERIALS (for 1 flower and 1 leaf)
  PETALS: Pink or white double crepe paper
  STAMENS: Yellow and brown double crepe paper
  LEAF: Green double crepe paper
  1 piece of wire (#26) wrapped with green tape, 4 in. long
  1 piece of wire (#18)
  4 pieces of wire (#30), 8 in. long
  Light green floral tape
  Glue

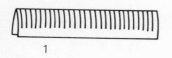

From the pattern on page 129, cut out 1 set of petals and 1 leaf. For the stamens, cut out 1 strip of pattern A from the yellow crepe and 1 strip of pattern B from the brown crepe.

Fold the stamen strip lengthwise in two with the front surface of the paper outside and cut 1/8 in. slits up to 1/4 in. from its lower edge (figure 1). Repeat the same procedure with the brown stamen strip.

Stick a piece of wire (#26) onto the back of the leaf about 1/2 in. from the tip (figure 2).

Wind tape to cover about 2 in. of the tip of the stem wire (#18) and hook it in the second slit from one end of the yellow stamen strip (figure 3). Roll it up tightly around the wire and cover this with the brown paper strip (figure 4).

Make small gathers along the base of the petal strip and wind it around the stamens with the front surface of the paper inside. Twist wire (#30) around the base and attach the stem wire to it with tape, winding it down the length of the stem (figure 5). About 3–4 in. below the flower, attach the leaf on a one-inch stalk and secure it with tape (figure 6).

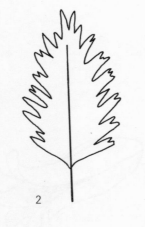

1

2

3

4

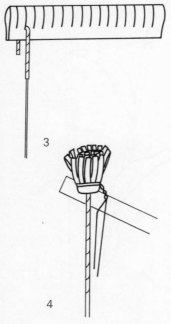

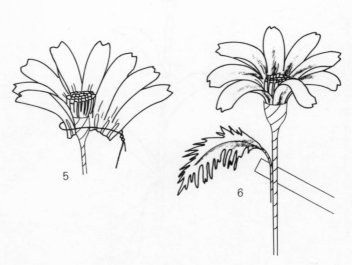

5

6

HYDRANGEA

MATERIALS (for 1 stem, 20 flowers and 5 leaves)
 PETALS: Blue, white, purple and pink double crepe paper
 STAMENS: 20 ready-made stamens
 LEAVES: Green double crepe paper
 5 pieces of wire (#22) wrapped with green tape, 7 in. long
 1 piece of wire (#18)
 29 pieces of wire (#30), 8 in. long
 Green floral tape

Working from the pattern on page 131, cut out 20 flowers and 5 leaves.

Make a small hole in the center of each flower (figure 1) and pass a stamen through it. Twist a piece of wire (#30) around the base of the flower and bind with tape about 4 in. down its length (figure 2).

Glue a taped wire (#22) down the center of the back of the leaf about 1 in. from its tip and bind the base with wire (#30) and tape (figure 3).

Gather all 20 flowers together in a bunch and bind them at their base with wire (#30), leaving a two-inch stalk. Attach the stem wire (#18) to the stalk and bind together with tape. About 2–4 in. below the flowers, fix 2 leaves on one-inch stalks to face each other and bind them with tape. Join the remaining leaves in the same manner at about 3–4 in. intervals (figure 4).

Note: The flowers may all be of the same color or can be varied according to your taste.

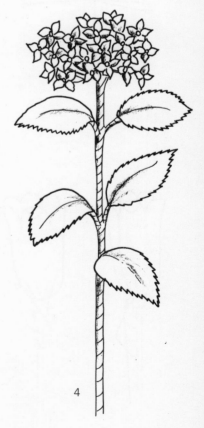

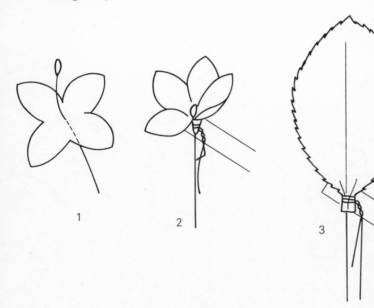

1

2

3

4

FOXGLOVE

MATERIALS (for 1 stem, 15 flowers, 5 buds and 20 leaves)
   PETALS AND BUDS: Purple or pink double crepe paper
   STAMENS: 45 ready-made stamens
   LEAVES: Green double crepe paper
   1 piece of wire (#18)
   42 pieces of wire (#30), 4 in. long
   Green floral tape

Following the pattern on page 132, cut out 15 sets of petals, 5 buds, 10 large leaves and 10 small leaves.

Twist wire (#30) around the center of 3 stamens, bend them in half and bind the base with wire (#30) and tape (figures 1 and 2). Curl the edges of the petals outward by pressing firmly with your fingertips and glue the ends together to make a cylindrical shape (figure 3). Place the stamens inside the cylinder, arranging them so that their tips protrude above the petals,

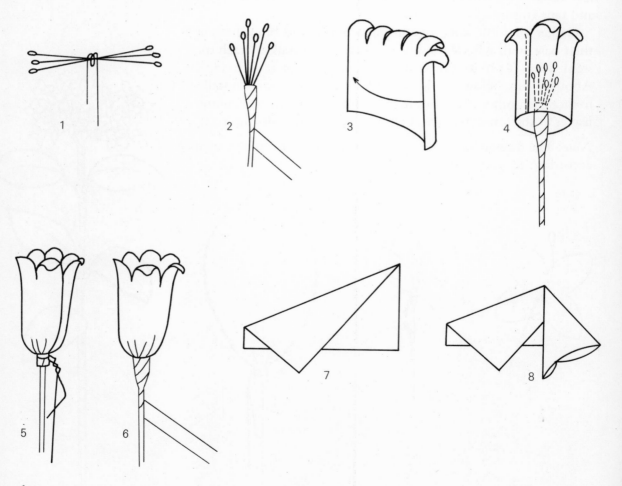

and bind the base with wire (#30) and floral tape (figures 5 and 6).

To make the buds, first fold the paper strips as shown in figure 7, then roll them up from the right-hand side and bind with wire (#30) and tape (figures 8, 9 and 10).

The base of the leaf is also bound with wire (#30) and tape (figures 11 and 12).

Take a piece of stem wire (#18) and attach 5 buds to it with tape at intervals of 1–1 1/2 in. (figure 13). Attach the flowers underneath the buds in the same manner, on one-inch-long stalks made from wire (#30), and bind with tape. The last flower should be placed 10–12 in. from the tip of the main stem. Underneath the flowers, attach the small leaves first and then the large leaves (figure 14).

Note: The buds, flowers and leaves should be arranged in a corn shape so that the foxglove can be viewed from all angles. If you wish to make the bouquet shown in the color plate on page 22, vary the number of buds and flowers on each stem.

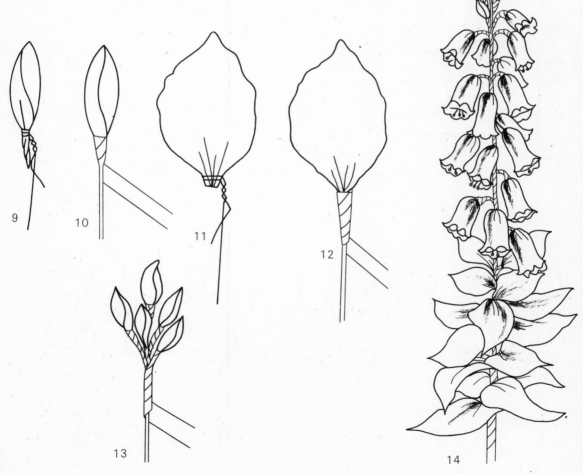

9

10

11

12

13

14

SNAPDRAGON

MATERIALS (for 1 stem, 10 flowers, 8 buds and 20 leaves)
  PETALS AND BUDS: Yellow, red or pink double crepe paper
  BUDS AND LEAVES: Green double crepe paper
  1 piece of wire (#18)
  40 pieces of wire (#30), 8 in. long
  Green floral tape

From the pattern on page 131, cut out 10 sets of petals and 5 buds from the yellow, red or pink crepe, and cut out 3 buds and 20 leaves from the green paper.

Stretch the center of each petal set sideways (figure 1) to produce a convex effect on the central piece and a concave effect on the petals on either side of it (figure 2). Make gathers at the base of each petal set and fold it in three in a zigzag pattern

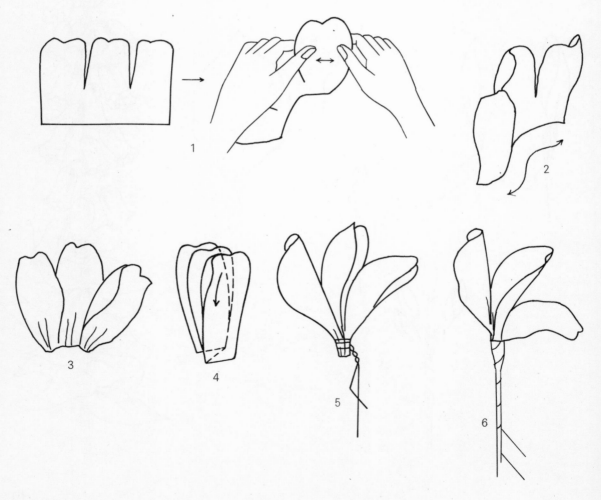

(figures 3 and 4). Then turn the petal at one end right around on its head, so that the front surface of the crepe is turned inside. Twist wire (#30) around its base and wind tape over it (figures 5 and 6).

Fold the green and red squares for the buds as shown in figures 7 and 8, then roll them up. Bind the base with wire and tape (figures 9 and 10).

To make the leaves, bind the base of each leaf with wire (#30) and floral tape (figure 11). Attach a piece of wire (#18) to the base of a bud with tape, and as you wind the tape downward, add to the main stem the green buds first, followed by buds of the same color as the snapdragon, and finally the flowers themselves. Allow 1/4–1/2 in. between each bud and flower and arrange them into a corn shape.

About 3 in. below the last flower, attach the leaves with tape (figure 12) in the same manner as the flowers.

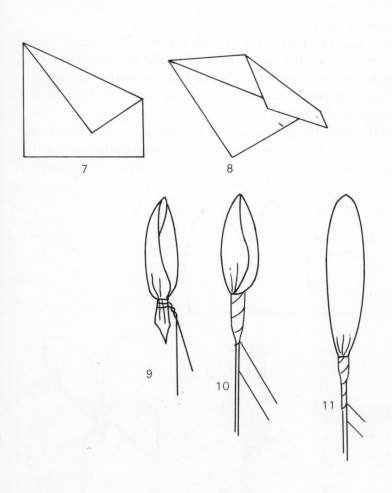

GLADIOLUS

MATERIALS (for 1 stem, 4 flowers, 2 half-opened flowers, 2 buds, 2 tight buds and 2 leaves)

PETALS AND BUDS: Orange single crepe paper

CALYX, TIGHT BUDS AND LEAVES: Green double crepe paper

2 pieces of wire (#22) wrapped with green tape, 12 in. long

2 pieces of wire (#18)

24 pieces of wire (#30), 8 in. long

Green floral tape

Double-faced tape

Following the pattern on page 133, cut out 12 sets of petals from the orange crepe (8 sets for the flowers, 2 sets for the half-opened flowers and 2 sets for the buds). Also cut out 16 sepals for the calyx and 2 tight buds from the green crepe. For the leaves, cut out 2 strips (2 in. × 10 in.) and 2 more strips (2 in. × 8 in.) from the green crepe.

To make the tight buds, stretch the middle of each paper strip sideways to create a concave effect and roll it up from one end with the front side out. Twist a piece of wire (#30) around the base and cover with tape (figures 1 and 2). Repeat the process to make 2 tight buds.

For the buds the procedure is the same as above. Stretch the center of each paper strip to produce a concave effect and roll it up from one end (figure 3). Then attach 2 sepals to the base of

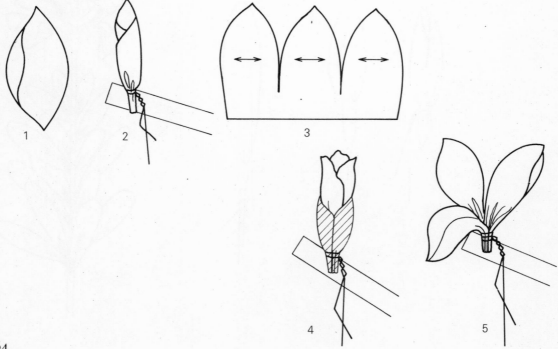

each bud, arranging them to face each other, and bind them with wire (#30) and tape (figure 4).

To make the half-opened flowers, roll a petal strip with the front surface inside and bind the base with wire (#30) and tape (figure 5). Take 2 sepals, fix them to the base of the flower and bind with wire and tape in the same way as for the buds. Repeat the process with the second flower.

For each of the 4 flowers in full bloom, use 2 sets of petals to make 1 half-opened flower first (see above), and enclose this with another set so that the petals alternate. Bind with wire (#30) at the base and cover with tape. Arrange 2 sepals about 1 in. below the flower and bind them at the base with wire and tape (figures 6 and 7).

To make the leaves, follow figure 8 and place wire (#22) vertically on the back surface of the green paper strip in the center of the left-hand side, 1/2 in. from the tip. Stick double-faced tape over it and fold in half to stick them together. Then cut out the leaves according to the pattern.

To attach the flowers to the stem, begin with the tight buds first, attaching each to a piece of wire (#18) by binding the base with tape (figure 9). The second tight bud is attached in the same way to the stem about 2 in. lower, followed by the first bud, the second bud, the half-opened flowers, the flowers in full bloom and lastly the leaves. Note that the distance between the flowers should get progressively shorter toward the bottom of the main stem.

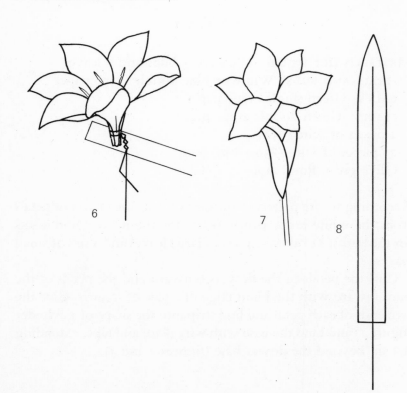

6

7

8

9

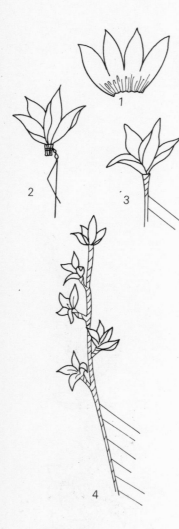

FORSYTHIA

MATERIALS (for 1 stem and 20 flowers)
   PETALS: Yellow single crepe paper
   1 piece of wire (#18)
   20 pieces of wire (#30), 8 in. long
   Twig green floral tape
   Tissue paper

Cut out 20 sets of petals according to the pattern on page 134.
   Make gathers at the base of each petal strip (figure 1) and join the two ends together to form a circle. Then bind the base with wire (#30) (figure 2). This first flower belongs to the tip of the stem, so do not tape the wire; but make the other 19 flowers in the same way and then bind the wire with tape (figure 3).
   Attach the first flower to the tip of the stem wire (#18) with tape and wind it down the rest of the stem. Cover the stem with strips of tissue paper and then wind more tape over it, at the same time attaching the flowers to the stem with floral tape at intervals of 1–2 in. all the way down the stem (figure 4).

Note: Should a thicker stem be desired, use more than 1 piece of wire (#18).

GENTIAN

MATERIALS (for 1 stem, 6 flowers, 5 buds and 8 leaves)
   PETALS AND BUDS: White or blue double crepe paper
   CALYX: Green single crepe paper
   LEAVES: Green double crepe paper
   2 pieces of wire (#18)
   29 pieces of wire (#30), 8 in. long
   Olive green floral tape   Glue

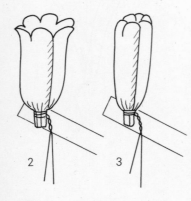

According to the pattern on page 134, cut out 11 sets of petals from the white crepe paper (6 sets for the flowers and 5 sets for the buds), 11 calyxes, 4 sets of large leaves and 4 sets of small leaves.
   Curl the petals of the flowers outward and the petals of the buds inward with the blunt edge of a pair of scissors. Glue the two ends of each petal and bud strip into the shape of a cylinder (figure 1) and bind the base with wire (#30) and tape, extending it 1 in. beyond the flower base (figures 2 and 3).

Enclose the lower portion of the flower and bud with the calyx, and bind with wire (#30) and tape (figure 4).

Assemble 3 flowers and 2 buds to form a spray and bind them at their base with wire (#30). Attach 2 pieces of wire (#18) to it and wind tape around the join (figure 5).

At the base of the first spray of flowers, wrap a set of small leaves with the front surface of the paper inside and enclose with a set of large leaves. Then bind them with wire (#30) and tape, winding it down the stem (figure 6).

Following the same procedure, make another spray of 2 flowers and 2 buds, and attach it 4 in. below the first one with wire (#30) and tape. Then, as before, enclose the flower base with the calyx, small and large leaves, and bind with wire (#30) and tape. The third spray of flowers is joined to the stem in the same way, about 4 in. below the second spray (figure 7).

Next attach a small leaf followed by a large leaf around the main stem, 4 in. below the third spray, and bind with wire and tape wound down the length of the stem.

Note: When more than one stem is arranged in a container as shown in the color plate on page 26, the number of flowers and buds in each spray can be varied, as well as the number of sprays on each stem or the number of leaves at the lower end of the stem.

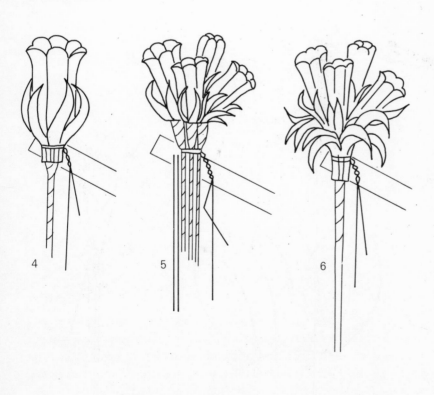

4

5

6

7

RHODODENDRON

MATERIALS (for 1 stem, 2 flowers, 3 buds and 5 leaves)
   PETALS AND BUDS: Pink double crepe paper
   STAMENS: 20 ready-made stamens
   LEAVES: Green and brown double crepe paper
   5 pieces of wire (#22), 7 in. long
   5 pieces of wire (#18)
   16 pieces of wire (#30), 8 in. long
   Green floral tape   .Double-faced tape
   Tissue paper   Crayon   Glue

Following the pattern on page 136, cut out 21 petals (12 for the flowers and 9 for the buds) and 5 strips (5 in. × 1 1/2 in.) from the green crepe and 5 from the brown paper.

Place a piece of wire (#22) in the center of the back of the green strip, 1/2 in. from the top, and stick it down with double-faced tape, applied over the entire back surface (figure 1). Then stick the brown crepe paper on top of it with the front surface outside and cut out the shape of the leaf according to the pattern.

Bend a piece of wire (#30) and twist it around the center of 4 stamens, then bend them in half and cover the base with tape (figures 2 and 3).

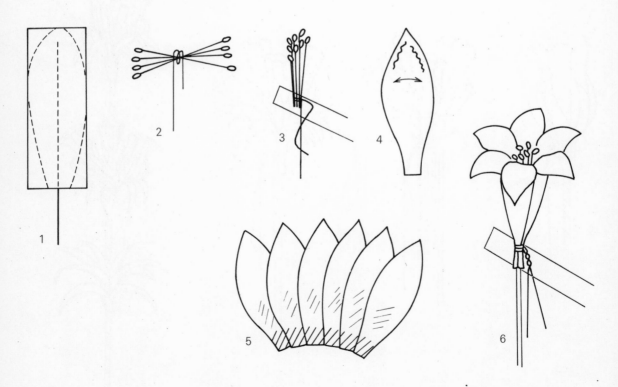

Stretch the petals to produce a convex effect (figure 4), and make a wavy pattern along their edges by twisting the rim with your fingertips (refer to *Basic Steps* on pages 10–12). Then glue 6 petals together as shown in figure 5 and shade the base of the petals with crayon the same color as the crepe paper. Roll up the petals in the shape of a trumpet, with the front surface of the paper inside, and glue the ends together. Then insert the stamens in the center and bind the base with wire (#30) and tape (figure 6).

To make the buds, glue 3 petals together as shown in figure 7, then follow the same procedure used for making the flowers, but this time roll the bud petals in the shape of a trumpet with the front surface outside. Place the stamens in the center and bind the base of the buds with wire (#30) and green floral tape (figure 8).

Assemble 2 flowers and 3 buds together and bind them with wire (#30). Attach 5 pieces of stem wire (#18) to their base with tape and wind it down the entire stem. Cover the stem with strips of tissue paper and once more with floral tape. While winding down with floral tape for the last time, add the leaves, starting with one leaf 1 in. below the flowers and then gradually increasing the interval between each subsequent leaf as shown in figure 9.

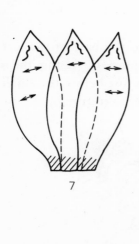

7

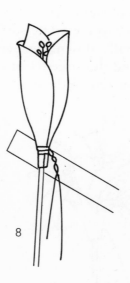

8

9

EDELWEISS

MATERIALS (for 1 flower and 2 sets of leaves)

    PETALS AND LEAVES: White and light green single crepe paper

    DISKS: 3–5 dried flowers (*yellow immortelles*)

    LEAVES: White and light green single crepe paper

    2 pieces of wire (#30), 8 in. long

    1 piece of wire (#20)

    Light green floral tape   Glue

According to the pattern on page 136, cut out 1 strip (2 in. × 4 in.) from the white crepe and another strip of the same size from the green crepe. Glue the two strips together and from this cut out the petals. Use the same method for the leaves, cutting out 1 strip (2 in. × 4 in.) for the large leaf from the white and green crepe, and one strip (1 1/4 in. × 4 in.) for the small leaf from both papers. After gluing each of the two pieces of the same size together, cut out the shape of the leaves.

Cut off all but 2 in. of the stems of the dried flowers and bind them together with wire (#30) and tape (figures 1 and 2).

Glue the two ends of each petal together into a cylindrical shape with the green surface outside and insert the dried flowers in the center, winding wire (#30) around the base.

Attach a piece of stem wire (#20) to the flower base and wind tape around it (figure 4).

Apply glue to the white surface of the base of the leaf and wind it spirally down the stem (figure 5). Using the same method, wind the large set of leaves just below the small one and cover the rest of the stem with tape (figure 6).

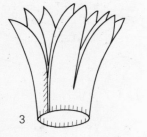

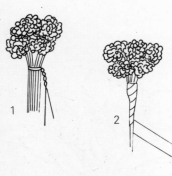

DAISY

MATERIALS (for 1 flower)
  PETALS: White single crepe paper
  STAMENS: Yellow single crepe paper
  1 piece of wire (#28) wrapped with white tape
  2 pieces of wire (#24)
  3 pieces of wire (#18)
  Light green floral tape   Absorbent cotton

Following the pattern on page 135, cut out 1 set of petals and 1 strip for the stamens.

Stretch the center of the stamen strip to give it a convex effect and place a piece of absorbent cotton, the size of a ping-pong ball, in the center. Wrap it up in the paper and twist a piece of wire (#24) around the neck. Attach 3 pieces of wire (#18) to the base with tape, extending it about 3 in. beyond the base (figures 1, 2 and 3).

Insert a piece of wire (#28) in between the folded petal strip and crush it along its base to make gathers. Wrap the petals around the stamens and pull the wire tightly around the base, twisting it several times (figures 5 and 6). Wind wire (#24) over the base of the petals about 1 in. from the bottom and attach 3 pieces of stem wire (#18) to it. Bind with floral tape, wound down the entire stem (figures 7 and 8).

Open out the petals and, as a finishing touch, stretch each petal sideways as shown in figure 9.

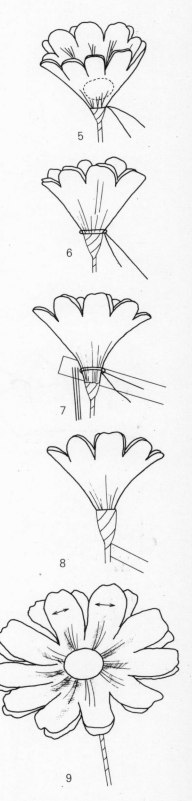

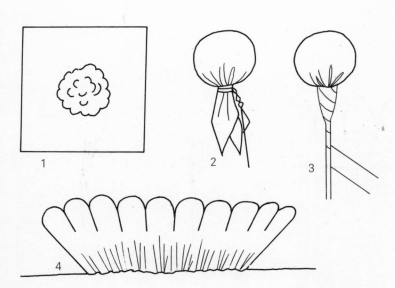

BOUVARDIA

MATERIALS (for 1 stem, 5 flowers, 5 buds and 10 leaves)

PETALS, COROLLAS AND BUDS: Red or white double crepe paper

LEAVES AND CALYXES: Green double crepe paper

1 piece of wire (#18)

32 pieces of wire (#30), 8 in. long

Light green floral tape   Glue

According to the pattern on page 137, cut out 10 sets of petals (5 for the flowers and 5 for the buds), 10 corollas, 1 calyx, 5 large leaves and 5 small leaves.

Stretch the petals sideways to create a convex effect (figure 1) and, with the front surface outside, roll up the petals and bind the base with wire (#30), then cover with floral tape (figure 2). All 5 sets of petals are made in the same manner.

The strip for the corolla is also stretched sideways to produce

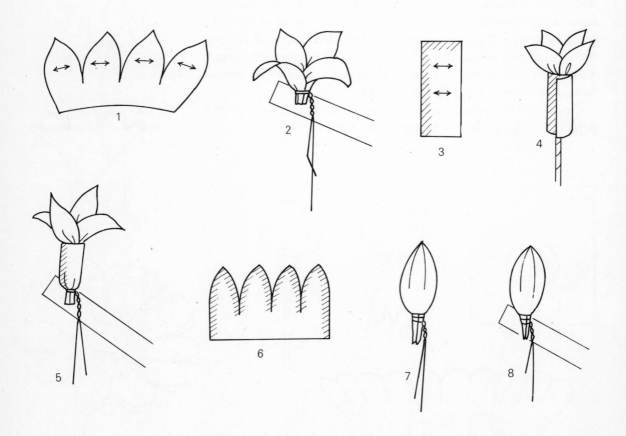

this convex effect (figure 3) and, after gluing one side of the paper, wrap it around the base of the flower (figure 4). Cover the wire below the corolla with tape (figure 5).

For the buds, glue the edges of the strip as shown in figure 6 and stick the petals together (figure 7). Bind the base with wire (#30) and tape (figure 8). Repeat the same procedure as above to attach the corollas to the base of the buds as shown in figure 9.

Make gathers at the base of the leaf and bind with wire (#30) and tape.

Gather 5 flowers and 5 buds in a bunch and bind them together with wire (#30) and floral tape about 1/2 in. below the corollas. Next wrap the calyx around this and bind with wire (#30). Attach a piece of wire (#18) to the base of the calyx with tape and wind it down (figures 10 and 11).

About 1–1 1/2 in. below the calyx, attach a large leaf on a half-inch stalk with tape, followed by a small leaf at an interval of 1–1 1/2 in. Attach the remaining 8 leaves in the same way (figure 12).

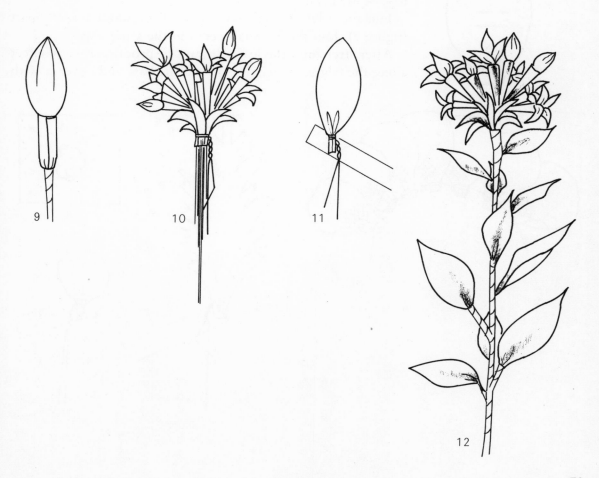

9

10

11

12

ANEMONE

MATERIALS (for 2 flowers and 6 leaves)
  PETALS: Red, pink or yellow double crepe paper
  DISKS OF FLOWERS: Black single crepe paper
  STAMENS: 40 black ready-made stamens
  LEAVES: Green double crepe paper
  2 pieces of wire (#18), 12 in. long
  16 pieces of wire (#30), 8 in. long
  Green floral tape
  Absorbent cotton   Tissue paper
  Crayon

Cut out 7 large petals, 12 small petals, 2 strips for the disks and
6 leaves according to the pattern on page 138.

Following figure 1, stretch the petals in the directions indicated by the arrows to make a concave effect in the center. Then
twist the paper along the edges to produce a wavy effect. With
a crayon the color of the petal, shade the marked area at the
base of the petal.

Join the 7 large petals with wire (#30) about 1/8 in. apart
(figure 2). Join the 12 small petals in the same way.

After stretching the leaf sideways to produce a wavy effect
along the edges, twist wire around the base and cover it with

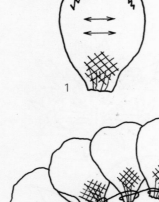

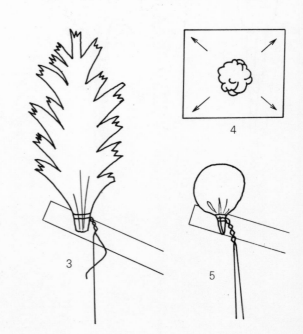

74

tape (figure 3). Stretch the black strip for the disk diagonally to make a hollow shape in the center. Place absorbent cotton in the hollow and make a ball about 1/2 in. in diameter. Twist wire tightly around the neck of the ball and cover it with tape (figures 4 and 5).

Take 20 stamens and bind the middle with wire (#30). Then place the disk in the center and arrange the stamens to surround it evenly. Bind the base with wire (#30) and tape (figures 6, 7 and 8). Make 2 stamens.

Surround the stamens with a set of 7 linked petals and bind with wire (#30). Attach the stem wire (#18) to the base of the flower with tape and wind it down the rest of the wire. Cover it with a strip of tissue paper 1/2 in. wide, wound spirally down, and then finish off with floral tape.

About 2 in. below the flower, attach 2 leaves facing each other with tape (figure 9). Similarly attach another leaf 3–4 in. below the first set. Wrap the remaining stamens with the 12 linked petals, binding them together with wire (#30). The stem wire (#18) is attached with tape and covered with tissue and floral tape. The same process as above is repeated to attach the 3 leaves to the stem.

Note: In an arrangement of many flowers, variation may be obtained by altering the space between the leaves from 1–4 in.

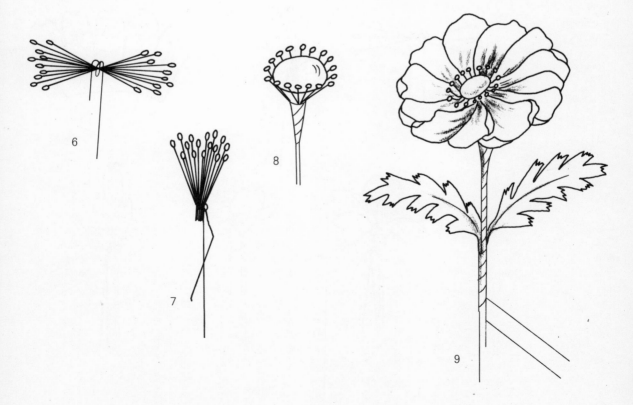

6

7

8

9

CHERRY BLOSSOM

MATERIALS (for 1 stem, 3 flowers, 4 buds and 3 leaves)
  PETALS AND BUDS: Pink single crepe paper
  STAMENS: 9 ready-made stamens
  CALYXES AND LEAVES: Green single crepe paper
  16 pieces of wire (#30), 4 in. long
  1 piece of wire (#22)
  1 piece of wire (#20)
  Brown floral tape
  Tissue paper   Glue

According to the pattern on page 138, cut out 7 sets of petals (3 sets for the flowers and 4 for the buds), 7 calyxes and 3 leaves.

Take 3 stamens, twist wire (#30) around the center, bend them in half, then bind the base with one end of the wire and cover with tape (figures 1 and 2).

Stretch the center of each petal to produce a convex effect (figure 3), wrap the petal strip around the stamens and bind with wire and tape (figure 4). Glue the calyx strip around the base of the flower and wind tape around its base (figure 5).

The strips for the buds are also stretched sideways and then

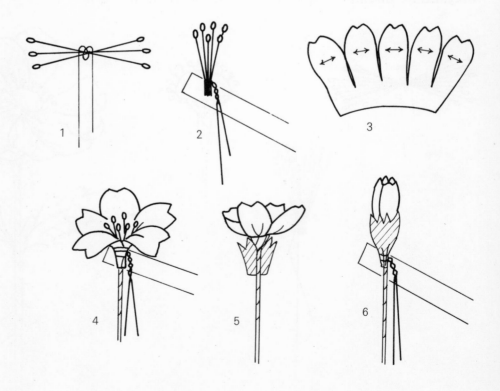

rolled and bound at the base with wire (#30) and tape. Wrap the calyx strip around the base of the bud and bind with wire and tape (figure 6).

The 4 buds are then combined on a stalk with wire (#30), and the 3 flowers are bunched with wire (#30).

The leaves are rolled up from one end and bound at the base with wire (#30). Arrange 2 leaves side by side at slightly differing heights and attach them together with wire (#30). At the base, attach a piece of stem wire (#22) and wind about 2 in. of tape around it. Attach the stalk of 4 buds to the stem with tape, allowing for 1 in. of stalk between the stem and the join. Wind tape 1–2 in. further down the stem and attach the flower stalk in the same manner. To thicken the flower stalk, add another piece of wire (#20) to the join where the flowers are bound together and wind tape over it, followed by tissue paper and more tape.

Note: If preferred, more leaves can be attached to the stem as shown in figure 8. Flowers and buds can be added, according to your taste, to the same stem. To achieve a more natural effect, a small branch of a cherry tree can be used instead of the wire stem. The cherry blossoms can be attached to the twig with wire that has been bound with brown floral tape and tied around the natural branch.

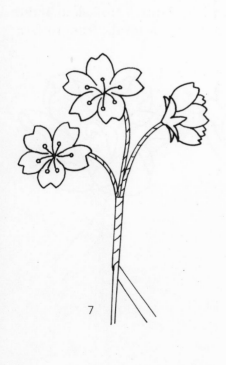

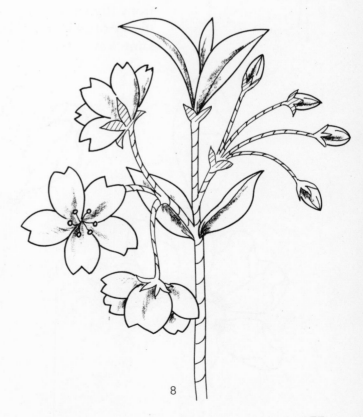

GARDENIA

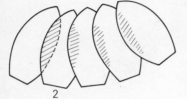

MATERIALS (for 1 stem, 1 flower, 1 half-opened flower, 1 bud
and 5 leaves)

PETALS AND BUD: White double crepe paper

CALYXES AND LEAVES: Green double crepe paper

2 pieces of wire (#18)

12 pieces of wire (#30), 8 in. long

Green floral tape

Tissue paper   Glue

According to the pattern on page 139, cut out 10 A petals (5
for the flower and 5 for the half-opened flower), 6 B petals,
1 strip for the bud, 3 A leaves, 3 B leaves, 2 A calyxes and 1 B
calyx.

Stretch the center of each petal as shown in figure 1 and stretch
the calyxes sideways to create a convex effect. Glue 5 A petals
together (figure 2) to make the half-opened flower and roll
them up from one end, gathering in the tips to close up at a
point. Twist wire (#30) around the base and cover with tape
(figures 3 and 4). Then wrap the A calyx around it, with the
front surface outside, and bind with wire (#30) and tape.

To make the flower, curl the edges of the petal toward the
front (figure 5) and join 6 B petals, 1/4 in. apart, with wire
(figure 6) and wrap them around the A petals (rolled up in the
same way as for the half-opened flower) with the front surface

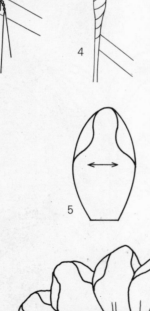

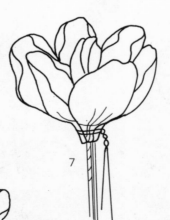

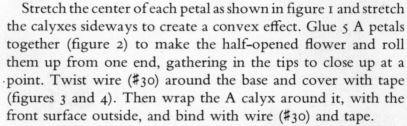

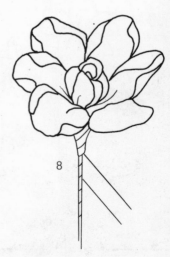

inside. Bind with wire (#30) and floral tape (figures 7 and 8).

Wrap the B calyx around the base of the flower and bind it with wire (#30) and tape (figure 9).

To make the bud, fold the strip as in figures 10 and 11, with the front surface of the paper outside, and roll it up from one end, then bind with wire (#30) and floral tape (figure 12). Enclose this with the A calyx and bind with wire (#30) and tape (figure 13.).

For the leaves, bind the base of the A and B leaves with wire (#30) and tape (except for the A leaf used at the tip of the stem) as shown in figure 14. The leaf for the tip of the stem is rolled up from one end and fixed with wire (#30) and tape at its base. Attach 2 pieces of stem wire (#18) to the base of this leaf with tape and wind it down the entire length. Then cover it with a doubled strip of tissue paper 1 in. wide and bind once more with floral tape. While winding the tape down the stem, attach the bud, flowers and leaves.

This is done by fixing the bud beside the leaf at the tip with tape, followed by the leaves and flowers at intervals of 2 in. (figure 15).

If another stalk is required, place a rolled-up leaf or bud on the tip of a piece of wire (#30) and add on leaves and flowers underneath it at two-inch intervals; then attach all this to the main stem with wire (#30). If the join does not look smooth enough, wrap more tissue paper over it and cover once more with floral tape.

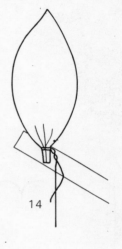

14

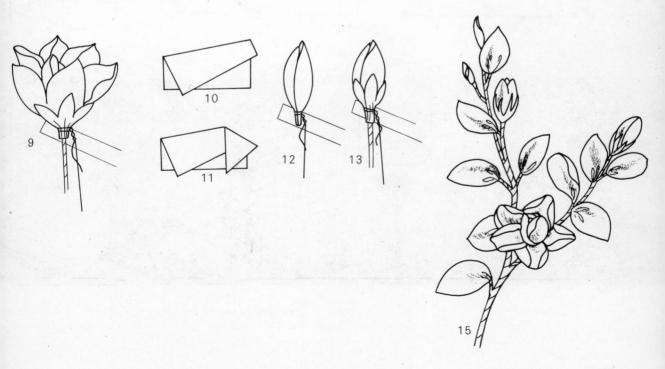

9

10

11

12

13

15

LILY OF THE VALLEY

MATERIALS (for 1 stem, 4 flowers and 2 leaves)
PETALS: White double crepe paper
STAMENS: 4 dried flowers (*Helichrysum*)
LEAVES: Green double crepe paper
7 pieces of wire (#30), 8 in. long
10 pieces of wire (#18)
Green floral tape   Tissue paper   Glue

Cut out 4 sets of petals and 2 leaves according to the pattern on page 144.

Make slits about 1/2 in. long and at intervals of 1/2 in. along the lower edge of the petal strip (figure 1). Stretch this sideways to create a convex effect (figure 2) and curl each petal outward. Glue the ends of the crepe together, with the front surface outside, to make a cylindrical shape (figure 3). Insert 1 dried flower in the center and bind the base with wire (#30) as shown in figures 4 and 5.

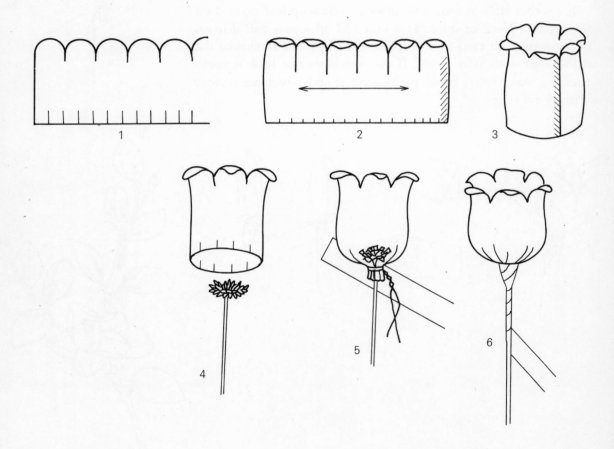

Attach 1 stem wire (#18) to each of 3 flowers and wind tape about 4 in. down the stem. Cover the stem with tissue paper first and then wind more tape around it (figure 6). For the last flower, attach 3 pieces of wire (#18) to its base and bind with tape, followed by tissue paper and more tape as shown in figure 7.

For the leaves, join 2 pieces of wire (#18) together by winding tape around them as shown in figure 8. Bend this wire into the shape of a horseshoe and glue it onto the back of the leaf (figure 9).

About 8 in. below the first flower, join a second flower to the main stem on a three-inch stalk. Wind tape about 6 in. down the stem and then cover this with tissue paper strips and more floral tape. Fix the third flower at an interval of 6 in. and bind it to the main stem with tape, followed by a covering of tissue paper and more tape. Join the last flower to the stem at an interval of about 5 in. (figure 10).

Note: The leaves are not attached to the flower stem and can be arranged to your own liking.

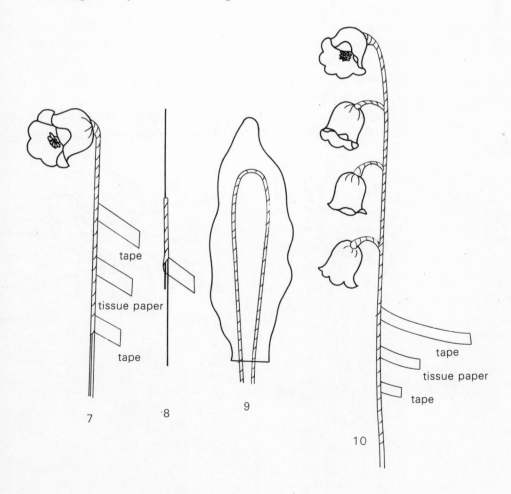

POMPON DAHLIA

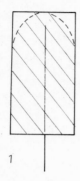

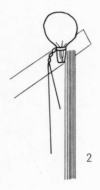

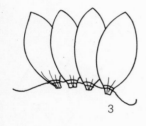

MATERIALS (for 1 stem, 1 flower and 2 leaves)
PETALS: Pink double crepe paper
DISK: Yellow single crepe paper
STAMENS: Yellow single crepe paper
CALYX AND LEAVES: Green double crepe paper
20 pieces of wire (#22) wrapped with white tape, 6 in. long
2 pieces of wire (#20) wrapped with green tape
4 pieces of wire (#28)
7 pieces of wire (#18)
3 pieces of wire (#30), 8 in. long
Green floral tape   Double-faced tape
Absorbent cotton   Tissue paper   Glue

Following the pattern on page 140, cut out 15 A petals, 12 B petals, 20 C petals, 1 strip for the disk from the yellow crepe and 8 sepals for the calyx from the green paper. For the leaves cut out 2 strips (10 in. × 5 in.) and 2 strips (10 in. × 4 in.) from the green paper.

To make the leaves, place wire (#20) down the center of the back of the strip and stick it down with double-faced tape applied over the entire surface (figure 1). Place the other strip of the same size over it and cut out the shape of the leaf according to the pattern.

Stretch all the petals sideways to give them a convex effect. Then make a ball of absorbent cotton, about 1 in. in diameter,

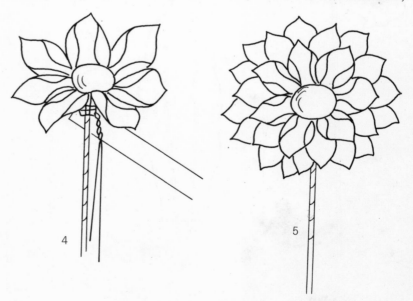

and cover it with yellow crepe. Twist wire (#30) around the neck and attach 7 pieces of stem wire (#18) to its base. Wind floral tape around them to hold them together, extending the tape about 3 in. down the wires (figure 2).

Join 15 A petals together with wire (figure 3) and wrap them around the disk with the front surface of the crepe outside. Bind the base with wire (#30) and tape, extending it 3 in. down the stem (figure 4). Join the 12 B petals in the same manner as above and arrange them around the A petals with the front surface of the paper inside. Bind the base with wire (#30) and tape (figure 5).

Glue wire (#22) down the center of the back of the C petals about 1/2 in. from the top and join all of them together with wire (#28), as shown in figure 6. Make a ring with the C petals by hooking one end of the wire to the other and wrap this around the A and B petals with the front surface of the paper inside. Bind the base with wire (#28) and wind tape down the whole length (figure 7).

Glue each of the 8 sepals around the base of the dahlia as evenly as possible (figure 8). To make the calyx, take each sepal and cut a slit at the base and cross the two flaps over to make the sepals concave in appearance (figure 9). When all the sepals are attached, wind tissue paper (1 in. wide) from the base of the calyx down the stem and cover once again with floral tape.

Note: In the color plate on page 33, the leaves are not attached to the main stem, but this can easily be done with wire (#30) if preferred.

8

9

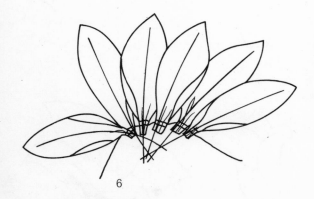

6

7

CACTUS DAHLIA

MATERIALS (for 1 stem, 1 flower and 2 leaves)
  PETALS: Yellow, brown, red or orange double crepe paper
  CALYX AND LEAVES: Green double crepe paper
  10 pieces of wire (#22) wrapped with tape the same color as
     the flower, 9 in. long
  2 pieces of wire (#20) wrapped with green tape
  5 pieces of wire (#18)
  3 pieces of wire (#30), 8 in. long
  Twig green floral tape   Tissue paper
  Double-faced tape   Glue

Working from the pattern on page 141, cut out 8 A petals, 6 B petals, 10 C petals and 6 sepals (for the calyx). To make the leaves, cut out 4 strips (10 in. × 5 in.) from the green crepe.

Stick a piece of wire (#20) down the center of the back of each leaf with double-faced tape over the wire only. Stick another strip over it and cut out the shape of the leaf (figure 1). Stretch the edges of each leaf with the fingertips to produce a wavy effect (figure 2).

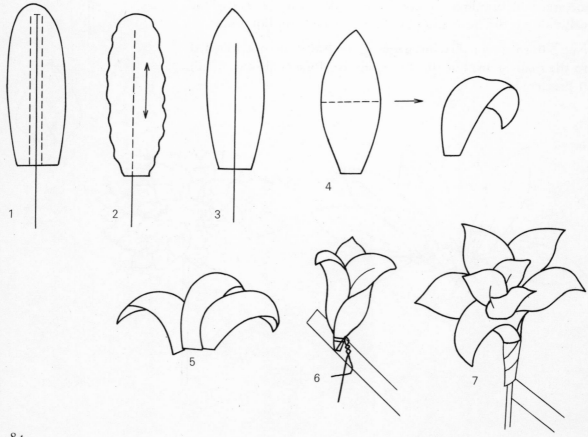

Glue a piece of wire (#22) down the center of the back of the C petals (figure 3). Curl the upper edges of petals A and B outward, toward the back of the paper, with the blunt edge of a pair of scissors (figure 4). Then arrange 3 A petals side by side as shown in figure 5 and roll them up, with the front surface inside, and bind the base with wire (#30) and tape (figure 6). ·The remaining 5 A petals are rolled in the same manner around them, followed by the 6 B petals and finally the 10 C petals (figures 7 and 8). Wind tape over the base, extending the tape 3 in. down the wire (figure 9).

Bind 5 pieces of wire (#18) onto the base of the flower with tape and cover with tissue paper strips 1 in. wide. Wind floral tape once more over the stem.

Glue together 6 sepals as shown in figure 10 and stick them around the base of the flower. Wind tape from the base of the calyx 3 in. down the stem (figures 11 and 12). Then attach the leaves to the stem with wire (#30) and cover the rest of the stem with tape.

Note: The leaves, however, need not be attached to the stem but may be arranged on separate stalks.

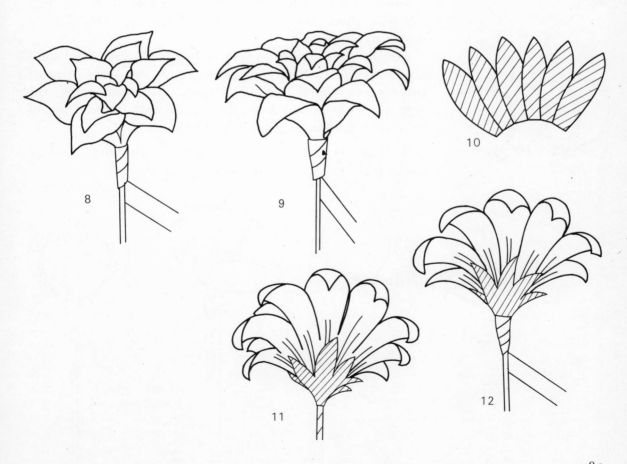

POPPY

Materials (for 1 flower)
  Petals: Orange single crepe paper
  Disk: 20 black ready-made stamens and 1 poppy pistil
  Stem: Green single crepe paper
  1 piece of wire (#18), 12 in. long
  4 pieces of wire (#30), 8 in. long
  Green floral tape   Tissue paper

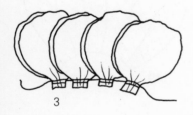

According to the pattern on page 145, cut out 8 petals and 1 stem.

Bunch 20 ready-made stamens together, twist wire (#30) around the center and bend them in half. Tighten the wire and cover it with tape. Insert the poppy pistil in the center of the stamens and bind the base with wire (#30) and tape (figure 1).

Place 2 petals on top of each other and stretch the center area sideways to produce a convex effect. Twist along the edges of the petal to create a wavy pattern (figure 2). Repeat the same process with the other petals.

Join the 4 petals with wire (#30) about 1/6 in. apart (figure 3) and wrap them around the stamens. Bind with wire (#30) as shown in figure 4.

Attach a piece of wire (#18) to the base of the flower and wind tape over the entire length. Then cover this with strips of tissue paper, 1/2 in. wide, and wrap it with the green stem strip. Both are wound down the entire length of the wire and fixed with floral tape (figures 5 and 6).

Note: Instead of the ready-made stamens, the disk could be made of either paper or ribbon with thin slits cut in it.

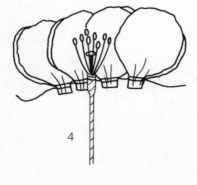

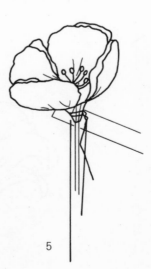

HYACINTH

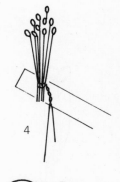

4

MATERIALS (for 1 stem, 25 flowers and 10 leaves)

   PETALS: Pink, blue and pale yellow satin ribbon, 3 in. wide
   STAMENS: 75–100 ready-made stamens
   LEAVES: Green satin velvet ribbon, 3 in. wide
   10 pieces of wire (#22) wrapped with green tape, 7 in. long
   27 pieces of wire (#30), 8 in. long
   1 piece of wire (#20)
   Green floral tape   Double-faced tape   Glue

Working from the pattern on page 145, cut out 25 sets of petals, 5 strips (1 1/2 in. × 6 in.) and 5 other strips (1 1/2 in × 5 in.) for the leaves.

Place a piece of wire (#22), 1/2 in. from the top, down the center of one half of the leaf strip (figure 1) and stick it down with double-faced tape to cover one half of the entire strip. Fold the other half over it and cut out the leaf.

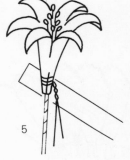

5

Glue the ends of the petal strip as shown in figure 2, with the front surface of the ribbon inside, to make a conical shape. Curve each separate petal outward (figure 3), using the blunt edge of a pair of scissors. Then bend 3–5 stamens in half and bind them at the base with wire and tape (figure 4). Place the stamens in the center of the flower and bind with wire (#30) and tape around the base (figure 5). Repeat the same procedure with all the other flowers except for one. Bind this one to the tip of the stem wire (#20) with tape.

As you wind the tape down the main stem, attach the flowers, on one-inch stalks, to the stem at intervals of 1/2 in. (figure 6). The flowers should be tightly packed so that the stem is more or less invisible, and should be arranged in a corn shape as in figure 6. About 4 in. below the last flower, attach 10 leaves to the stem with wire (#30) and tape.

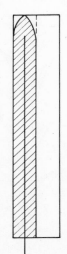

1

2

3

6

CARNATION

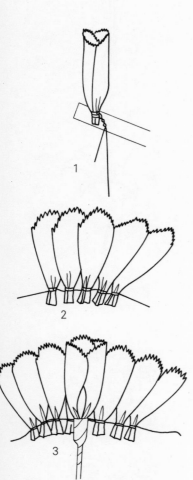

MATERIALS (for 1 stem, 1 flower and 6 leaves)
   PETALS: Pink silk *ombre* ribbon, 3 in. wide
   CALYX AND LEAVES: Green satin ribbon, 2 in. wide
   8 pieces of wire (#30), 8 in. long
   1 piece of wire (#20)
   Green floral tape
   Absorbent cotton   Glue

Working from the pattern on page 146, cut out 26 petals, 1 calyx and 6 leaves.

With figure 1 as a guide, make a center disk for the flower by rolling up 2 petals with the front surface outside and bind the base with wire (#30) and tape.

Next join 8 and 16 petals respectively with wire (#30), spacing them about 1/2 in. apart at the base (figure 2). Wrap the center disk of the flower first with the set of 8 petals, with the surface of the ribbon facing inward, and tie the base with wire and tape (figures 3 and 4). Then wrap the second set of 16 petals around it, with the surface inside, and fix at the base with wire (#30). Join the stem wire (#20) to it and cover with a thin piece of absorbent cotton about 1 in. long. Wind tape over the cotton to fix it to the stem (figure 5). Then glue the calyx to the base with tape (figure 6).

As you wind tape down the stem, attach 2 leaves to it with wire (#30). Arrange them on both sides of the stem to face each other, with the front surface of the ribbon outside (figure 7). The distance between the flower and the first set of leaves is about 2 in., but allow the space between the leaves to get progressively longer toward the bottom.

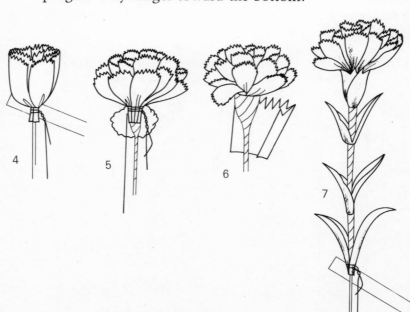

DAFFODIL

MATERIALS (for 1 flower and 3 leaves)
  PETALS: White satin ribbon, 3 in. wide
  CORONA: Yellow satin ribbon, 1 1/2 in. wide
  STAMENS: 2 ready-made stamens
  LEAVES: Green satin ribbon, 1 1/2 in. wide
  1 piece of wire (#18), 12 in. long
  5 pieces of wire (#30), 8 in. long
  3 pieces of wire (#22), 9 in. long
  Green floral tape   Tissue paper   Double-faced tape

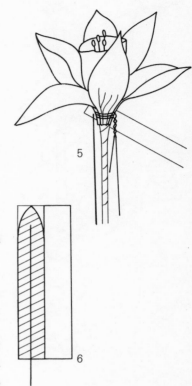

Working from the pattern on page 147, cut out 6 petals, 1 corona (the trumpet-shaped part in the center of the petals), 2 strips (1 1/2 in. × 6 in.) and 1 strip (1 1/2 in. × 8 in.).

Bend 2 stamens in half, twist wire (#30) around the base and wind tape over it (figure 1).

Glue along the ends of the corona and stick them together with the front surface of the ribbon outside. Place the stamens inside the corona and bind with wire and tape (figures 2 and 3).

Join the 6 petals together with wire (figure 4), 1/8 in. apart, at the base and wrap them around the corona with the front surface of the ribbon inside. Bind the base with wire (#30) and attach the stem wire (#18) to it with tape, winding it down its entire length (figure 5). Cover the stem with tissue paper strips, 1/2 in. wide, and finish off with floral tape.

Stick a piece of wire (#22) down the back of each leaf, placing it in the center of the left-hand half, 1 in. from the top. Apply double-faced tape over the shaded area (figure 6) and fold the other half of the ribbon over it. Cut out the shape of the leaf following the pattern. Then arrange 1 large leaf and 2 small ones at the base of the stem and attach them with wire (#30) and tape (figure 7).

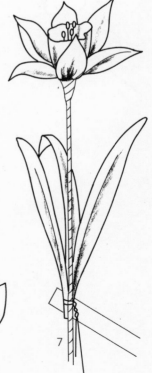

Note: The method of arranging a bunch of daffodils to the best effect is to work with the flowers and the leaves separately, placing them piece by piece into a block of Styrofoam.

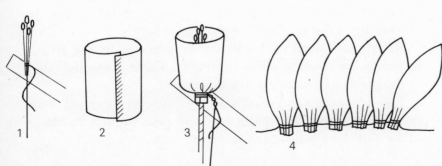

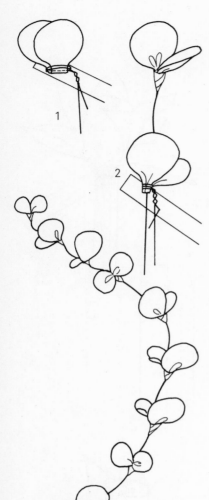

A EUCALYPTUS FANTASY

MATERIALS (for 1 stem and 40 leaves)
LEAVES: Acetate or satin ribbon (any color), 1 1/2 in. wide
1 piece of wire (#20)
20 pieces of wire (#30), 8 in. long
Green floral tape

Working from the pattern on page 151, cut out 10 large and 10 small leaves.

Fold 1 leaf in half with the front surface of the ribbon turned inside and bind the base with wire (#30) (figure 1). Wind tape over it, extending it about 2 in. down the wire. Then add the second leaf to it by inserting the wire between the folded leaf and binding the base with wire (#30) and tape, again extending it 2 in. down the wire (figure 2). The third leaf is fixed in the same way, but after binding the third leaf with wire (#30) add another piece of wire (#20) to make the stem and then cover it with tape. Attach the rest of the leaves in the same way (figures 1, 2 and 3). The large and small leaves can be arranged to suit your own taste.

EVENING PRIMROSE

MATERIALS (for 1 stem, 2 flowers, 2 buds and 6 leaves)
PETALS AND BUDS: Pink or yellow acetate ribbon, 2 in. wide
STAMENS: 40 ready-made stamens
LEAVES: Green acetate ribbon, 3 in. wide
1 piece of wire (#18), 12 in. wide
1 piece of wire (#30)
Green floral tape

Using the pattern on page 148, cut out 12 petals (8 for the flowers and 4 for the buds) and 6 sets of leaves.

Stretch each petal in the directions indicated by the arrows to produce a concave effect (figure 1). Twist along the edges of the petals to produce a fluted pattern.

Take 10 stamens and wind wire (#30) around the center, bend them in half and bind with wire and tape (figures 2 and 3). Make 4 of these bunches of stamens.

Take 4 petals and link them together with wire (#30) at intervals of 1/8 in. Wrap them around one bunch of stamens, with the front surface inside, and bind the base with wire (#30) and tape (figures 4 and 5).

To make the buds, wrap 2 petals around one bunch of stamens, with the front surface outside, and bind with wire (#30) and tape (figures 6 and 7).

Gather 2 flowers and 2 buds and bind them together at the base with wire (#30). Then attach a piece of wire (#18) for the main stem with green floral tape. At the base of the bunch of flowers, attach 2 sets of leaves, with the front surface of the ribbon outside, and bind them with wire (#30) and tape. Attach the other set of leaves 2–4 in. below the first set in the same manner, and the third set the same distance below the second (figure 8).

Note: A better effect can be produced by putting 3–4 sets of leaves on a stem, adding 1 or 2 buds to the second and third sets of leaves as shown in figure 8.

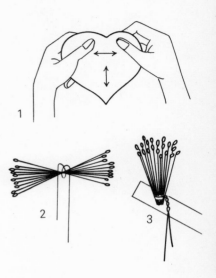

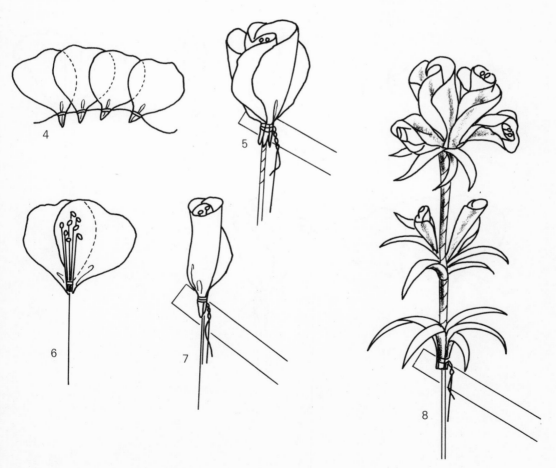

ROSE

MATERIALS (for 1 flower, 1 bud and 4 sets of leaves)
  PETALS AND BUD: Deep red silk *ombre* ribbon, 3 in. wide
  LEAVES: Green velvet ribbon with graded colors, 3 in. wide
  2 pieces of wire (#18), 12 in. long
  21 pieces of wire (#30), 8 in. long
  Green floral tape

Working from the pattern on page 149, cut out 17 petals (11 for the flower and 6 for the bud) from the red silk ribbon and 12 leaves from the green velvet ribbon.

To make the 2 cores of the flower and bud, curl the upper right-hand edge of 2 petals toward the front surface of the ribbon (figure 1). For all the remaining 15 petals, curl both edges toward the back as shown in figure 2.

The cores of the flower and its bud are made by rolling 1 petal from the uncurled end and binding the base with wire (#30).

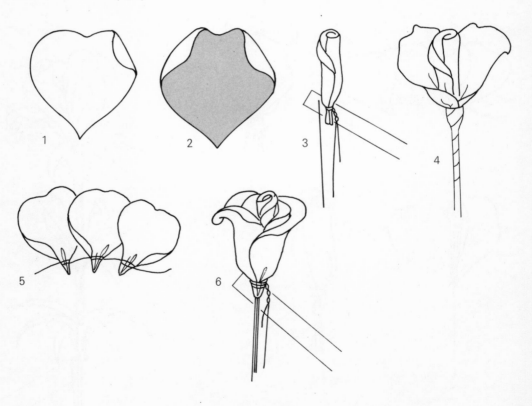

92

Attach a piece of stem wire (#18) to the core and bind it with tape (figure 3). Enclose the rolled core with 2 petals facing each other with the front surface of the ribbon inside. Secure it at the base with wire (#30) and tape (figure 4). Join 3 petals with wire (#30), about 1/4 in. apart, and wrap them around the core with the front surface inside. Fix the base with wire and tape (figure 6). Make 2 of the above, one for the flower and one for the bud.

Join the remaining 5 petals with wire (#30), 1/4 in. apart, as shown in figure 7 and wrap them around the 3 linked petals with the front surface inside. Bind the base with wire (#30) and cover with tape (figure 8).

Take a leaf, twist wire (#30) around the base of it and cover with tape, extended 2 in. beyond the base. Join 3 leaves in the manner shown in figure 9. Attach 1 leaf stalk 2–4 in. below the base of the flower and another stalk 2–3 in. below that, binding with floral tape.

The remaining leaf stalks for the bud are attached in the same way to the stem, underneath the bud.

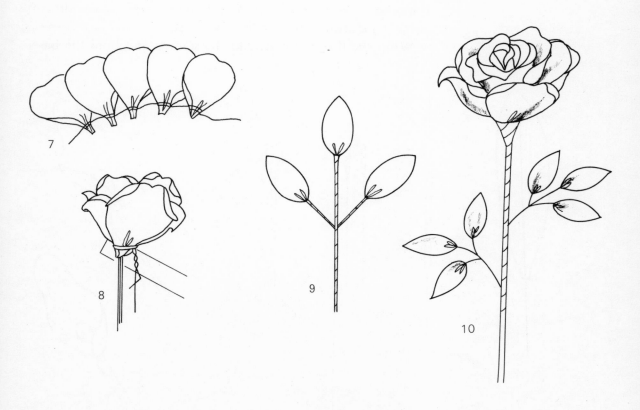

MOTH ORCHID

MATERIALS (for 1 stem, 5 flowers and 4 leaves)
   PETALS, CALYX AND LIPS: Pink double crepe paper
   LEAVES: Green double crepe paper
   5 pieces of wire (#26), 8 in. long
   4 pieces of wire (#26) wrapped with green tape, 6 in. long
   1 piece of wire (#18)
   10 pieces of wire (#30), 8 in. long
   Yellow and light green floral tape
   Tissue paper

Working from the pattern on page 148, cut out 10 petals, 5 lips, 15 sepals (for the calyx) and 4 leaves.

Glue a piece of wire (#26) wrapped with green tape down the center of the back of each leaf about 1/2 in. from the tip (figure 1).

To make the stamen, wind about 1 in. of tape around the middle of a piece of wire (#26) and bend it in the shape of a horseshoe (figures 2 and 3). Wind yellow tape to a width of about 1 in. around the center (figure 4).

Wrap the flower lip around the stamen and bind the base

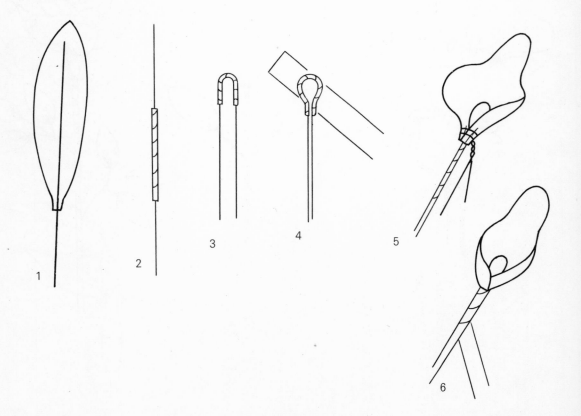

with wire and light green floral tape as shown in figures 5 and 6.

Stretch the center of each petal as shown in figure 7 and bind the base with wire (#30) and tape (figure 8). Make the flower by attaching 2 petals, followed by 3 sepals, around the lip and bind the base with wire as shown in figure 9. Wind tape around the stalks of 4 of the 5 flowers (except the one at the tip of the stem), extending it about 3 in. down the wire.

Attach a piece of stem wire (#18) to the base of the flower for the tip of the stem and bind it with tape, winding it down the stem. About 4 in. below the first flower, attach the second one with tape on a stalk 2 in. long. Attach the remaining flowers in the same manner at intervals of 3–4 in.

About 6 in. below the last flower, place 2 leaves facing each other and join them to the stem with wire (#30); place the second pair of leaves about 4 in. below the first. Pad the stem between the 2 sets of leaves with tissue paper to make it more oval in appearance, and cover with floral tape. Pad the stem below the second set of leaves with tissue paper strips and cover with tape.

Note: If the stem is too short, it can easily be lengthened by joining another piece of wire (#18) to it.

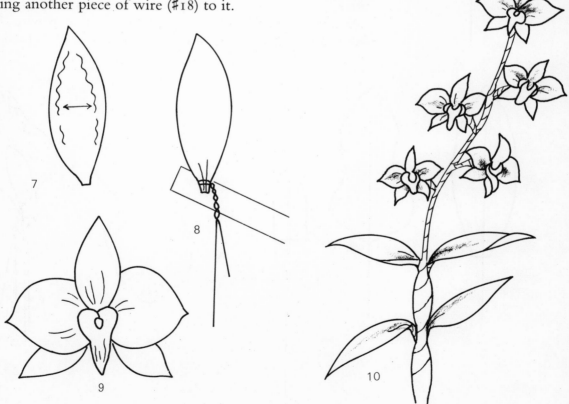

OLD WORLD ORCHID

MATERIALS (for 1 stem, 3 flowers, 2 buds and 6 leaves)
PETALS AND BUDS: Olive green velveteen ribbon, 2 in. wide
LEAVES: Green velveteen ribbon, 1 1/2 in. wide
24 pieces of wire (#26) wrapped with green tape, 4 in. long
1 piece of wire (#26), 3 in. long
9 pieces of wire (#30), 8 in. long
6 pieces of wire (#20)
3 pieces of wire (#18)
Olive green floral tape   Tissue paper
Double-faced tape   Crayon   Glue

Using the pattern on page 149, cut out 21 petals (6 are for the buds), 3 A lips and 3 B lips to make the flower. To make the leaves, cut out 2 strips each in the following sizes: 16 in. × 1 1/2 in., 8 in. × 1 1/2 in. and 20 in. × 1 1/2 in.

Attach a piece of wire (#20) to the back of the leaf in the center of the left–hand half as shown in figure 1 with double-faced tape, and apply it over half the cut strip. Fold the other half over it and cut out the shape of the leaf according to the pattern.

At the back of the petals and lips, glue a piece of wire (#26) wrapped with green tape as shown in figure 2. Use crayon to

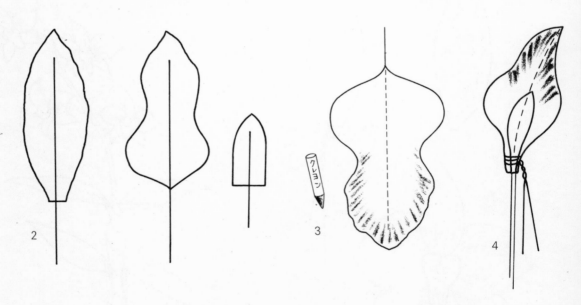

color the shaded area of lip A on the front surface (figure 3) and arrange lip B to face it, binding them at the base with wire (#30) and tape (figure 4).

Enclose the lips with 5 petals, with the front surface inside, and bind the base with wire (#30) and tape, extending it 2 in. down the wire (figures 5 and 6).

To make the bud, place 3 petals with the front surface of the ribbon facing out and bind the base with wire (#30), as shown in figure 7. Make the other bud in the same way, but this time cover the base with tape first, followed by tissue paper strips and tape once again to cover about 3 in. of the wire. Attach 3 pieces of stem wire (#18) with tape to this and wind it down the stem.

Attach the buds and flowers on two-inch stalks to the stem at intervals of 3–5 in. with tape (figure 8). If the stem looks too thin in proportion to the stalks, adjust this by winding tissue paper over it and covering with tape once again. When the last flower is attached, wind tissue paper down the entire stem and cover it with tape.

The 6 leaves are attached to the stem at its base with wire (#30) and tape.

Note: If the length of the stem wire is too short, join a second piece of wire (#18) to it.

97

MAGNOLIA

MATERIALS (for 1 stem, 3 flowers and 2 buds)
   PETALS: Dark red velvet ribbon, 3 in. wide
   BUDS: Gray satin ribbon, 3 in. wide
   STAMENS: Yellow velvet ribbon, 3 in. wide
   CALYX: Brown satin ribbon, 3 in. wide
   18 pieces of wire (#24) wrapped with white tape, 6 in. long
   16 pieces of wire (#30), 8 in. long
   9 pieces of wire (#18)
   Twig green or brown floral tape
   Tissue paper   Glue

Working from the pattern on page 150, cut out 18 petals, 2 buds, 3 stamens and 15 sepals (for the calyx).

Take a piece of wire (#30) and wind floral tape about 2 in. down its tip and bend it as shown in figure 1. Hook this into the second slit of the stamen strip and roll it spirally down the wire. (figure 2). Bind the base with wire and tape.

To the back of each petal, glue a piece of wire (#24) down the center, 1/2 in. from the top (figure 3), then wrap 3 petals, with the front surface of the ribbon outside, around the stamens and bind with wire and tape (figure 4). Then surround this with

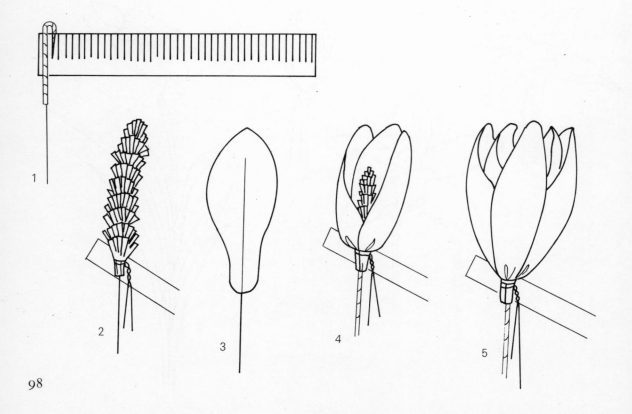

3 petals; arranging them in an alternating pattern as shown in figure 5.

Glue 3 sepals to the base of each flower, with the front surface of the ribbon outside, and then attach wire (#18) to its base with tape, extending it 4 in. down the wire. Cover the entire length of the wire with tissue paper, 1/2 in. wide, and wrap tape around it once more (figure 6).

To make the buds, fold the strip of gray satin ribbon with the front surface outside (figure 7) and roll it up from the right-hand side as shown in figure 8. Bind the base with wire (#30) and tape (figure 9). Glue 3 sepals to the base of each bud in the same manner as above, and cover with tissue paper and tape (figure 10).

Next combine the flowers and buds as shown in figure 11 by attaching 4–5 pieces of wire (#18) to the base of one of the buds with tape, winding it down the entire length. Cover it with tissue paper and tape. About 4 in. below the first bud, attach the second bud with wire (#30) on a stalk 2 in. long. Repeat the same process and join the flowers at intervals of 3–5 in. to the main stem with wire (#30).

Note: The stalk without either bud or flower in figure 11 is made by putting 3–5 pieces of wire (#18) about 4 in. long together and covering them with tape, tissue paper and tape.

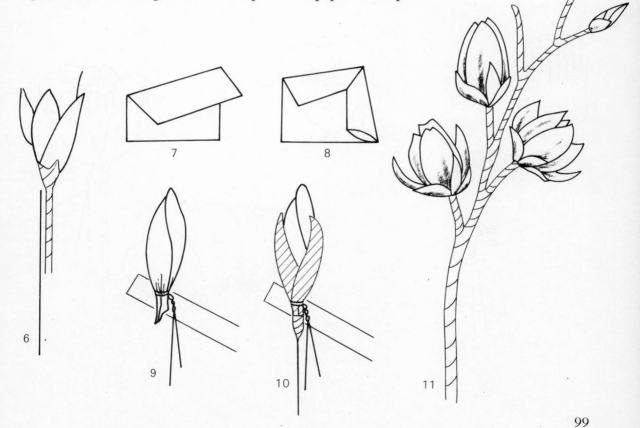

CAMELLIA

MATERIALS (for 1 flower, 1 bud and 2 leaves)
PETALS AND BUD: White velveteen ribbon, 3 in. wide
STAMENS: Yellow velveteen ribbon, 3 in. wide
LEAVES: Green velveteen ribbon, 3 in. wide
2 pieces of wire (#26) wrapped with green tape, 5 in. long
5 pieces of wire (#30), 8 in. long
Twig green floral tape

Cut out, according to the pattern on page 151, 11 petals (3 for the bud), 1 A leaf, 1 B leaf and 2 strips for the stamens.

Curl the top edge of the stamen strip inward (figure 1) with the blunt end of a pair of scissors, apply glue to the ends of the strip and stick them together in a cylindrical shape. Wind wire (#30) around the base and cover it with tape (figure 2).

Stretch the petals in the directions indicated by the arrows to produce a concave effect on the front surface (figure 3).

Make the bud by joining 3 petals, 1/2 in. apart, with wire (#30) and wrap them around the stamens with the front surface inside (figure 4). Bind the base with wire and tape (figure 5).

To make the flower, repeat the same process of joining 3 petals together, wrapping them around the stamens with the

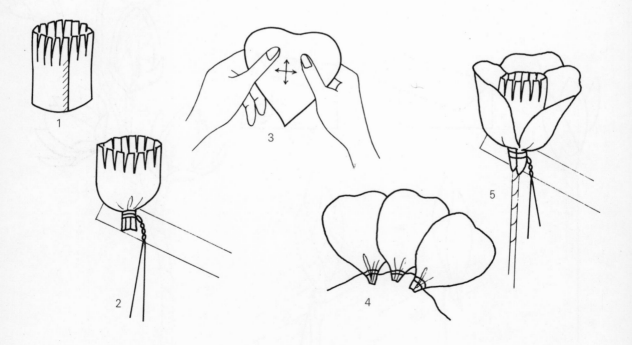

front surface inside, then binding the base with wire and tape. Next join 5 petals in the same way as above, 1/4 in. apart, and wrap them around the other petals with the front surface inside (figure 6). Bind the base with wire (#30) and tape, wound down the entire stem (figure 7).

Glue wire (#26) down the center of leaves A and B about ·1/2 in. from the tip (figure 8).

Note: In the color plate on page 40, artificial camellia stalks are fixed onto a dead branch with wire. To make the stalk, wind a piece of wire (#22) to the base of 1 leaf and cover with tape, extending it about 4 in. down the wire. About 3 in. from the base of the leaf, attach another leaf with tape, repeating the process to add 2 or 3 large and small leaves alternately on both sides of the stalk. The buds and flowers can be mingled among the leaves.

Join 3 or 4 stalks to the branch in the usual manner with wire and tape. To make a branch, take as many pieces of thick wire as necessary and bind them together with tape. Then wind strips of tissue paper to thicken it and cover this with more floral tape. Attach the stalks, flowers and buds to the branch with wire (#30) and cover the wire with tape. To give it a more natural effect, curve the tip of the branch and bend it slightly at the middle.

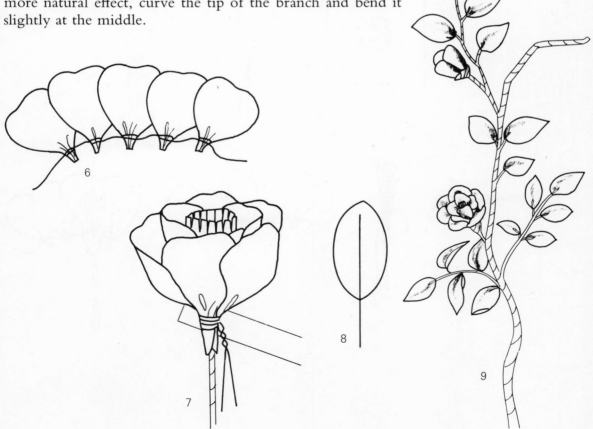

PEACH BLOSSOM

MATERIALS (for 1 branch, 3 flowers, 3 half-opened flowers and
            6 buds)
    PETALS AND BUDS: Pink satin ribbon, 3 in. wide
    CALYX: Green satin ribbon, 3 in. wide
    STAMENS: 18 white ready-made stamens
    33 pieces of wire (#30), 8 in. long
    1 piece of wire (#18)
    Brown or twig green floral tape
    Tissue paper   Absorbent cotton   Glue

Cut out, according to the pattern on page 152, 30 petals (5
petals are used to make 1 flower), 6 buds and 9 calyxes.

Stretch the four corners of the ribbon strip for the bud in
the directions indicated by the arrows and place some absorbent
cotton in the middle of the back of the material (figure 1).
Roll the cotton into a ball, twist wire (#30) around the neck
and cover it with tape (figure 2). Glue the calyx to the base of

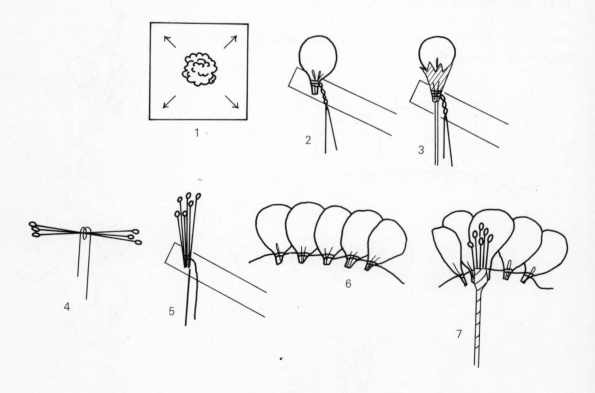

the ball and bind it with wire (#30) and tape (figure 3). Twist wire (#30) around the center of 3 stamens, bend them in half and bind the base with one end of the wire. Then cover with tape (figures 4 and 5). Make 6 sets of stamens.

In order to make a half-opened flower, link 5 petals on the same wire (#30) quite close to each other (figure 6) and wrap ·them around the stamens, binding the base with wire (#30) and tape (figures 7 and 8). Glue the calyx to the lower part of the flower and bind it with wire (#30) and tape (figure 9).

The flower in full bloom is made in the same way, with the 5 linked petals wrapped around the stamens and bound with wire (#30) and tape. But unlike the half-opened flower, it has no calyx and the petals are spread out more widely.

Attach wire (#18) to the base of a bud with tape and wind the tape down the entire stem. Cover the stem with tissue paper, cut in 1/2 in. strips, and then again with tape (figure 10). Add 1 or 2 buds and flowers to the stem with tape about 3 in. apart, as shown in figure 11, but shorten the intervals as you progress down the stem.

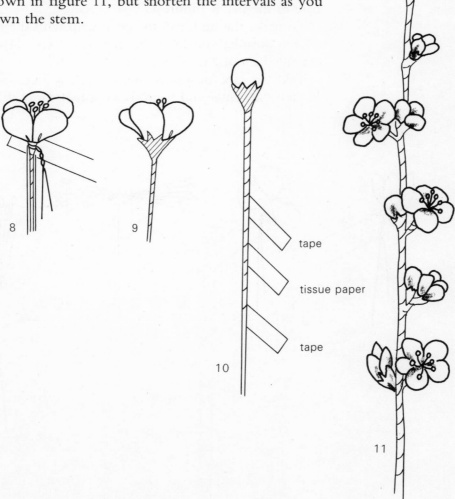

8

9

10

tape

tissue paper

tape

11

RAPE FLOWER BLOSSOM

MATERIALS (for 1 stem, 15 flowers, 5 buds and 7 leaves)
PETALS AND BUDS: Yellow satin ribbon, 3 in. wide
STAMENS: 45–50 ready-made rape flower stamens
LEAVES: Light green satin ribbon, 3 in. wide
33 pieces of wire (#30), 8 in. long
1 piece of wire (#18)
Light green floral tape
Tissue paper

Working from the patterns on page 152, cut out 20 sets of petals (5 of these are for the buds), 4 small leaves and 3 large leaves.

Roll up the ribbon strip for the petals with the front surface of the material turned inside and bind the base with wire (#30). Wind tape over the wire, extending it about 2 in. beyond the base of the petals (figure 1).

To make the bud, roll the petal strip with the front surface on the outside, and bind the base with wire (#30) and tape, extended about 2 in. (figure 2).

Take 20 rape flower stamens, hook a piece of wire (#30) around the center and bend them in half. Bind the base of the

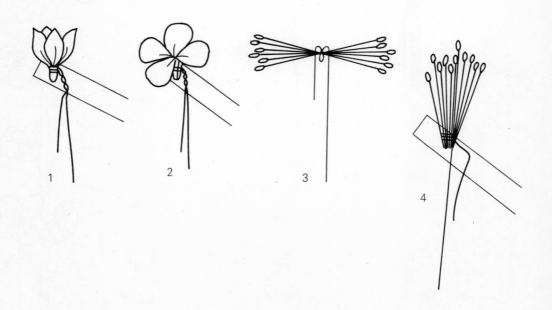

stamens with one end of the wire and cover it with tape, extending it about 2 in. (figures 3 and 4). In the same manner, make 5 smaller bunches with 5–6 stamens in each.

Arrange 15 flowers, 5 buds and 6 bunches of stamens together and, leaving about 1 1/2 in. for the stalks, bind them together with wire (#30). Attach a main stem wire (#18) to this with tape, extending the tape down the length of the stem (figure 5). Wind tissue paper, cut into strips about 1/2 in. wide, down the entire stem, then cover it once more with tape. The leaves are attached to the stem when floral tape is wound down it the second time.

Make the leaves by twisting the ribbon backward and forward along the edges to produce a wavy effect (see *Basic Steps*) and make gathers at the base. Attach them to the stem with wire (#30), with the front of the material inside, and wind tape over them (figure 6). Begin with the 4 small leaves on top, followed by the 3 large leaves underneath, at intervals of 1–2 in. (figure 7).

Note: If ready-made stamens for the rape flower are not available, you can make them with three-inch-long pieces of wire (#30). Twirl a little absorbent cotton around the tip of each piece of wire and cover with yellow floral tape. Make about 10 stamens for each flower and 4 for each bud.

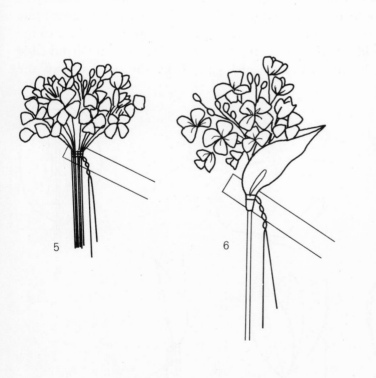

5

6

7

IRIS

MATERIALS (for 1 flower, 1 bud and 4 leaves)
  PETALS: Purple *ombre* and yellow satin ribbon, 2 in. wide
  BUD: Purple *ombre* ribbon, 3 in. wide
  LEAVES AND CALYXES: Green satin ribbon, 3 in. wide
  1 piece of wire (#26) wrapped with white tape
  4 pieces of wire (#20)
  6 pieces of wire (#30), 8 in. long
  6 pieces of wire (#18)
  Green floral tape   Handkerchief
  Tissue paper   Double-faced tape   Glue

Working from the pattern on page 152, cut out 3 A petals, 6 B petals (3 for the bud), 3 C petals from the purple ribbon and 3 D petals from the yellow ribbon. Cut the 4 calyxes from the green ribbon. Also cut out 2 leaves (1 1/2 in. × 16 in.) and 2 leaves (1 1/2 in. × 20 in.) from the green ribbon.

To make the leaves, place a piece of wire (#20) in the center of one half of the green satin ribbon (figure 1) and stick it down with double-faced tape, applied over half the leaf. Fold the other half over it and cut out the leaf.

Referring to figures 2, 3 and 4, fold the A petal in half with the front surface of the material outside. Prepare a handkerchief and insert the folded edge of the petal along the diagonal line where the handkerchief is folded. Then, pressing the base of the petal with the left hand, stretch by drawing the right-hand edge of the handkerchief toward you. Take the petal out of the

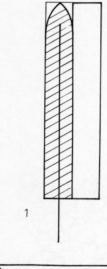

1

2

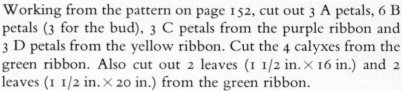

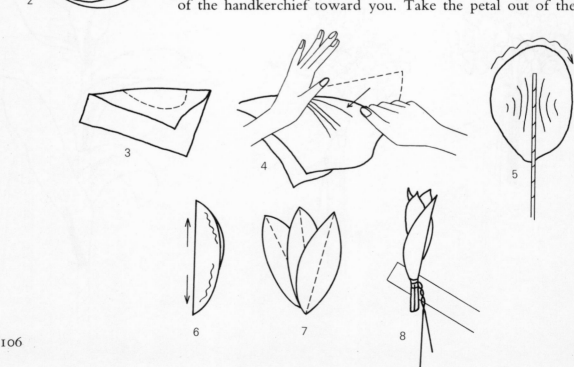

3

4

5

6   7   8

handkerchief, open it and twist along the edges with your fingertips to produce a wavy effect. Glue wire (#26) to the center of the back of the petal (figure 5). Fold the B petals lengthwise in half and stretch them in opposite directions as indicated by the arrows, twisting the edges to create a wavy effect, as shown in figure 6.

Place 3 B petals one on top of the other, as shown in figure 7, and roll them up from one end with the front surface outside. Bind the base with wire (#30) and tape (figure 8).

Place 3 C petals on top of 3 D petals and join their lower ends with wire (#30) 1/4 in. apart. Wrap these linked petals around the rolled B petals, with the front surface inside, and bind the base with wire (#30) and tape (figures 9 and 10). Under each D petal, attach an A petal and bind with wire (#30).

Add 3 pieces of wire (#18) to the base of the flower and cover them with floral tape, winding it down the entire stem (figure 11). Cut tissue paper 1/2 in. wide and wind it down the stem. Use tape again to cover the tissue paper. About 3 in. below the base of the flower, fix 2 calyxes with wire (#30), arranging them to face each other. Cover the wire with tape (figure 12).

To make the bud, place 3 B petals side by side with their edges slightly overlapping, roll them up from one end and bind the base with wire (#30) (figures 13 and 14). Attach 3 pieces of wire (#18) to the bud and fix them on with tape, winding it down the stem. The procedure of covering the stem with tissue paper and tape, as well as attaching the calyx underneath the bud, is the same as for the flower.

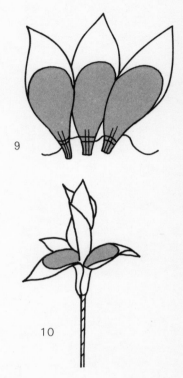

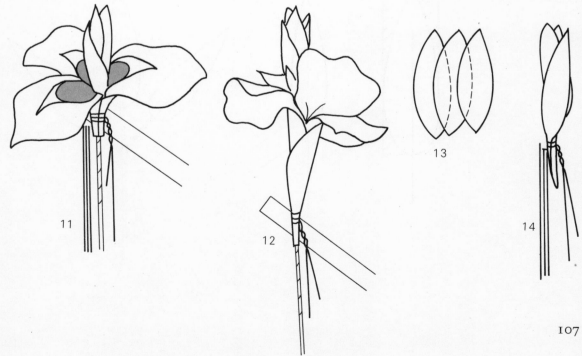

RED BAMBOO

MATERIALS (for 6 leaves)
   LEAVES: Orange *ombre* ribbon, 2 1/2 in. wide
   6 pieces of wire (#26) wrapped with white tape, 4 in. long
   Orange floral tape
   Double-faced tape

Cut out 6 rectangular strips (2 in. × 2/3 in.) and 6 other rectangular strips (2 1/2 in. × 5/6 in.).

Place wire wrapped with tape down the center of the back of 3 large strips, about 1/2 in. from the top. Stick it on with double-faced tape, covering the entire surface (figure 1). Stick the remaining 3 large strips over the tape and cut out the leaves according to the pattern on page 154.

Follow the same process for making the 3 small leaves. Cut the floral tape lengthwise in half and wind it down the leaf stalks (figure 2). Then combine 3 leaves, leaving about 1 in. of stalk for each leaf, and wind floral tape from the join downward (figure 3).

Note: The stalk shown in the color plate on page 41 is a Styrofoam cylinder used for display, which has been cut in two and covered with ribbon. Floral tape of the same color is twisted to form the joins. If Styrofoam is not available, thick paper rolled into a semi-circular form can be used instead.

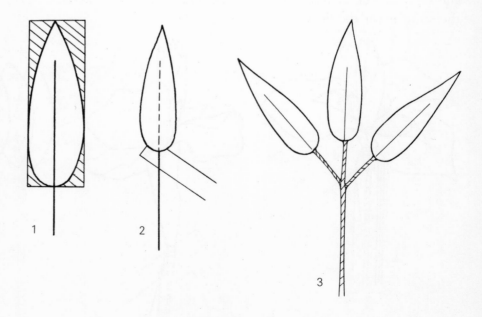

MAPLE

MATERIALS (for 1 twig)
    LEAF: Yellow, red or olive green acetate ribbon, 3 in. wide
    1 piece of wire (#28) wrapped with green tape, 4 1/4 in. long
    3 pieces of wire (#20)
    Brown floral tape   Glue

Cut out the leaf according to the pattern on page 154 and glue wire (#28) down the center of the back (figure 1).

Note: To make a maple branch, first prepare a number of two- or three-leafed twigs and attach them to the branch. The method of making a three-leafed twig is shown in figure 2. Attach a piece of wire (#20) to the base of the leaf, 1/2 in. from the top, and to this add 2 stems, 1 in. long, about 3 in. below the first leaf. Then attach the 2 leaves to the stems with tape (figure 3).

    If a longer branch is preferred, add on another piece of wire (#20) with tape. If a thicker branch is wanted, wrap several pieces of wire (#20) together with tape and cover them with tissue paper and again with tape. To make a two-leafed maple, refer to figure 2.

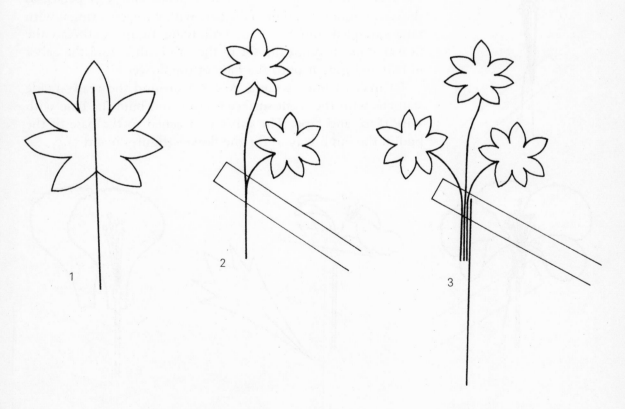

NASTURTIUM

MATERIALS (for 1 stem, 2 flowers, 2 buds and 5 leaves)
  PETALS AND BUDS: Yellow or orange satin ribbon, 3 in. wide
  STAMENS: 12 ready-made stamens
  CALYXES: Green satin ribbon, 2 in. wide
  LEAVES: Green velveteen ribbon, 3 in. wide
  15 pieces of wire (#26) wrapped with green tape, 5 in. long
  10 pieces of wire (#26) wrapped with white tape, 4 in. long
  8 pieces of wire (#30), 8 in. long
  1 piece of wire (#24)
  1 piece of wire (#22)
  Glue

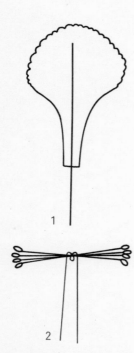

Following the pattern on page 154, cut out 8 A petals (4 for the buds), 6 B petals, 4 calyxes, 2 small and 3 large leaves.

To make the flowers, take 4 A petals and 6 B petals and glue wire (#26) down the center of the back, 1/2 in. from the tip (figure 1). Put 3 ready-made stamens together, twist wire (#30) round the center, then bend them in half and bind the base using one end of the wire. Cover the wire with tape, extending it another 3 in. (figures 2 and 3). To make 1 flower, enclose the ready-made stamens with 2 A petals and 3 B petals, as shown in figure 4, and bind the base with wire, covering it with tape extended another 3 in. Following figure 5, thread the flower stalk through the slit in the calyx, then fold the calyx in half and glue it onto the base of the flower.

To make a bud, wrap 2 A petals around the ready-made stamens with the front surface outside and bind the base with wire (#30) and tape. The calyx is attached to the base of the bud in the same way as for the flower (figures 6 and 7).

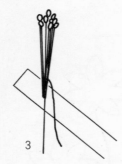

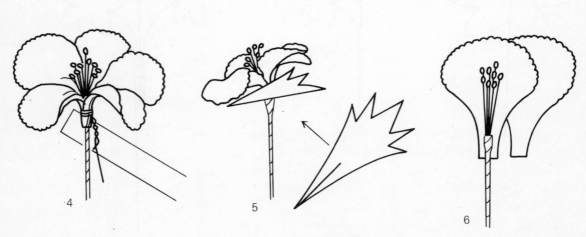

Join 3 pieces of wire (#26) according to figure 8 and wind tape from the join downward. One set of wires, which is glued to the back of the ribbon, is used to make each leaf (figure 9). Attach wire (#24) to the base of a large leaf with tape and, as you wind the tape spirally down, add the flowers, buds and leaves on stalks 1–2 in. long, at intervals of 2–3 in. as shown in figure 10. After attaching the first bud, join on another piece of wire (#22) to the main stem.

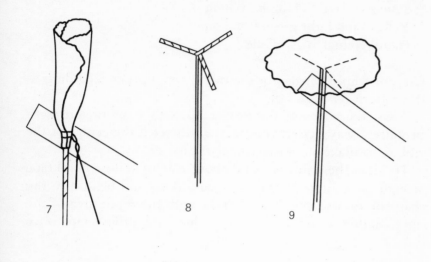

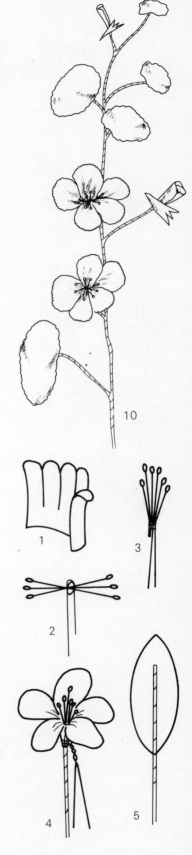

FLOWERET

MATERIALS (for 1 flower and 1 leaf)
  PETALS: White satin ribbon, 1 1/2 in. wide
  STAMENS: 2 or 3 ready-made stamens
  LEAF: Green velvet ribbon, 2 in. wide
  2 pieces of wire (#30), 8 in. long
  1 piece of wire (#26) wrapped with green tape
  Light green floral tape

Cut out 1 set of petals and 1 leaf according to the pattern on page 155.

Curl the edges of the petals backward, using the blunt end of a pair of scissors (figure 1). Wind a piece of wire (#30) around the center of 2 or 3 stamens, bend them in half, bind the base with one end of the wire and cover with tape (figures 2 and 3).

Make small gathers at the base of the petal strip and adjust the size of the base to fit snugly around the stamens with the front surface of the ribbon outside (figure 4).

Take the leaf and glue wire (#26) down the center of the back (figure 5), 1/2 in. from the tip.

CATTLEYA

MATERIALS (for 1 flower)

PETALS : White silk ribbon, 3 in. wide
CALYX : White satin ribbon, 2 in. wide
LIP : White velvet ribbon, 3 in. wide
5 pieces of wire (#26) wrapped with white tape, 6 in. long
1 piece of wire (#22), 8 in. long
2 pieces of wire (#30), 8 in. long
Yellow and light green floral tape
Handkerchief   Glue

Cut out 1 lip, 3 sepals (for the calyx) and 2 petals according to the pattern on page 155.

Twist the edges of the flower lip with your fingertips to produce a wavy effect (figure 1) and stretch the center of the ribbon to make a concave shape (figure 2).

To make the stamens, wind about 2 in. of yellow floral tape around the center of a piece of wire (#22) and bend it in the shape of a horseshoe. Make a ring with the taped area of the wire (figures 3 and 4) and cover this with yellow tape once

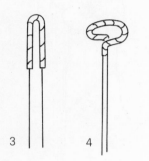

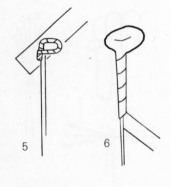

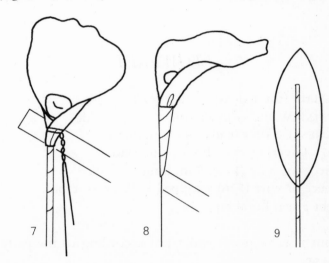

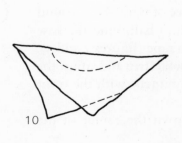

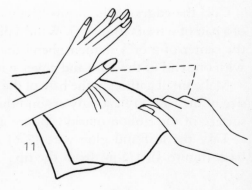

more (figures 5 and 6). Arrange the lip around the stamens with the front surface of the ribbon inside and bind the base with wire (#30) and tape (figures 7 and 8).

Glue a piece of wire (#26) down the center of the back of each sepal (figure 9).

Take a petal and fold it in half lengthwise and place it diagonally in a folded handkerchief as shown in figure 10. To make creases on the petal, place your left hand on the handkerchief and pull with your right hand toward you, squeezing and pressing the petal with the other hand (figure 11). Then glue a piece of wire (#26) down the center of the back of the petal (figure 12). Place the petals and sepals around the stamens and lip, with the front surface of the ribbon inside, and bind the base with wire (#30) and tape (figures 13 and 14).

Note: To make a bouquet of cattleyas and flowerets as shown in the color plate on page 44, first divide the shape of the bouquet in four separate parts (figure 15) and, after working on each section, bunch them together as shown in the sketch. The stems for the leaves and the flowerets are made by attaching wire (#22) to their bases with tape and then attaching the leaves and the flowerets to the wire according to your taste.

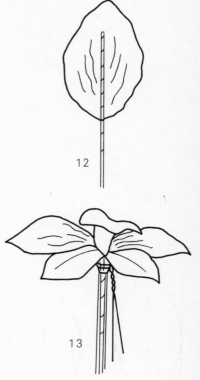

12

13

14

15

MATERIALS

PETALS: White velveteen and white silk ribbon, 3 in. wide
LEAVES: Green velvet ribbon with graded colors, 3 in. wide
55 pieces of wire (#24) wrapped with white tape, 6 in. long
27 pieces of wire (#24) wrapped with green tape, 8 in. long
40–50 pieces of wire (#30), 8 in. long
14–20 pieces of wire (#20)
Light green floral tape
Double-faced tape   Glue

With the pattern on page 156 as a guide, cut out 55 strips (4 in. × 1 1/2 in.) from the velveteen ribbon and 55 strips of the same size from the silky ribbon.

Place a piece of wire (#24) wrapped with white tape down the middle of the back of the velveteen strip about 1/2 in. from the top, and stick it down with double-faced tape applied over the entire back surface. Place the silk ribbon strip over this and cut out the petal according to the pattern (figure 1).

Cut out 10 large leaves and 11 small leaves. Glue wire (#24) wrapped with green tape down the center of the back of each leaf (figure 2).

Study figure 3 closely for the design of the finished bouquet. The bouquet is divided into 4 parts and each part should be worked separately, beginning with the central section, A.

Section A consists of 40 petals. Begin by making the core of the flower, putting 3 petals together with the front surface of

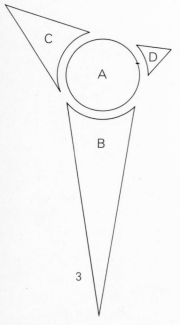

1   2

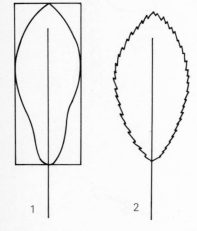

3

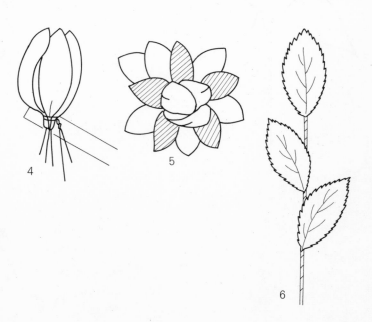

4   5   6

the ribbon outside (figure 4). Then bind the base with wire (#30) and cover with tape 2 in. down the wire. Next wrap 5 petals around this with the front of the ribbon inside and bind with wire and tape, extended 2 in. down the wire. Repeat the same procedure and wind all 40 petals around in progressively larger circles (figure 5). Then arrange 7 leaves, both large and small, around the base of the flower and bind the base with wire (#30) and tape.

To make section B, first attach wire (#20) to the base of a small leaf with tape wound 4 in. down the wire. Then attach the second leaf about 3 in. below this with tape (the leaf is also glued to wire [#20] first) as shown in figure 6. A little further below, attach a petal to a piece of wire so that it overlaps the leaf above it. Add 14 more petals in the same way with tape, all slightly overlapping. Then add on leaves here and there in the right places.

With section C, first attach a piece of wire to the base of a leaf with tape, extending it about 4 in. down the wire. About 3 in. below the first leaf, attach 2 leaves with tape on opposite sides of the stem. Add 3 more leaves in the same manner, increasing the intervals between the leaves as you go down (figure 7).

Section D is also made up of leaves only. Attach wire (#20) to 1 leaf with tape, winding it 3 in. below the stem. The second leaf is joined to the stem 2 in. below the first, and the third leaf about 1 in. below that (figure 8).

When all the sections are completed, assemble them as shown in figures 9 and 10, using wire and tape.

9

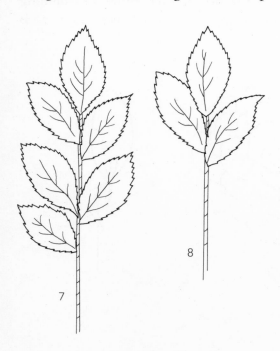

7

8

10

115

VICTORIAN ROSE

MATERIALS (for 1 stem, 2 flowers and 26 leaves)

   PETALS: Red acetate ribbon, 3 in. wide

   LEAVES: Green acetate ribbon, 3 in. wide

   Green acetate ribbon, 1 in. wide

   26 pieces of wire (#28), 8 in. long

   26 pieces of wire (#24), 8 in. long

   10 pieces of wire (#18)

   100 pieces of wire (#30), 8 in. long

   10 pieces of wire (#26), 8 in. long

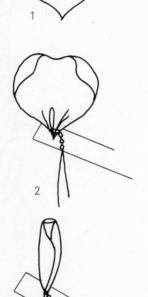

According to the pattern on page 156, cut out 40 A petals, 30 B petals, 10 C petals from the red acetate ribbon and 26 leaves from the green acetate ribbon.

Curl the edges of all the petals outward (figure 1), except for 2 that make the cores of the flowers, and bind the A and B petals with wire (#30) and tape. Bind the C petals with wire (#26) and tape (figure 2).

Take the 2 uncurled petals and roll them up, with the front surface outside, and bind the base with wire (#30) and tape (figure 3). Around each core, first arrange 3 A petals with the front surface inside and bind the base with wire (#30) and tape (figure 4). Now attach 5 A petals, next 11 A petals, then the B petals followed by the C petals. (The number of B and C petals used depends on the individual. But the general idea is to increase the number of petals in each layer, using just enough to enclose the center of the flower each time, and binding the base with wire [#30] and tape.) You need about 20 A, 20 B

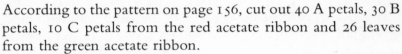

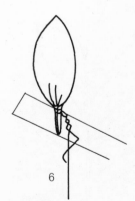

and 10 C petals for the larger rose, and 20 A and 10 B petals for the smaller rose (figure 5).

Bind the base of each leaf with wire (#28) and attach a piece of wire (#24) to its base with tape (figure 6). Arrange 3 leaves on each stalk, as shown in figure 7, and make 7 of these, including 1 branch of 5 leaves as shown in figure 8.

Join 5 pieces of wire (#18) to the base of the smaller rose with tape and wind tape 12 in. down to where the larger rose should be attached. Then cover with tissue paper, cut into one-inch strips. Attach the five-leafed stalk to the base of the flower with tape and wind tape down the entire stem.

About 8 in. below the first rose, attach the three-leafed branch with tape to the main stem, allowing for 4 in. of stalk between the leaves and the stem.

The larger rose and the 3 sets of leaf stalks are attached to the main stem with wire about 12 in. below the smaller flower. Use 5 pieces of wire (#18) and tape them to the base of the main stem and cover them with tape. (The entire stem should now be about 2 ft. 10 in. long.) Cover the tape with tissue paper and then with more tape. About 10 in. below the larger rose, attach 2 branches of leaves with tape.

As a final touch, wind green ribbon around the main stem, starting about 2 in. above the bottom, then turn the ribbon over and wind it up the stem. At the point where the larger rose is joined onto the stem, cut the ribbon off and glue the end to the main stem. Then begin winding from the smaller rose at the top downward and, when you reach the larger rose, cut off the ribbon and glue the end to the stem. Referring to figure 9, bend the main stem to give it a more natural effect.

9

tape

tissue paper

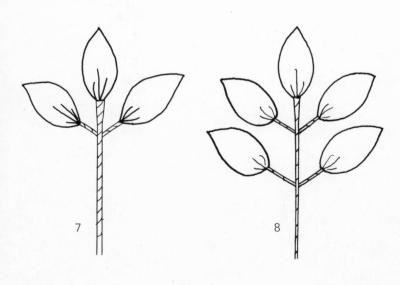

7

8

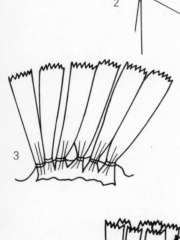

MATERIALS (for 1 stem, 1 flower and 2 leaves)
  FLOWER: Light and dark yellow acetate ribbon (or pale and
    dark pink acetate ribbon), 3 in. wide
  LEAVES: Green acetate ribbon, 3 in. wide
  6 pieces of wire (#24) wrapped with green tape, 6 in. long
  2 pieces of wire (#18)
  30 pieces of wire (#30), 8 in. long
  Twig green floral tape

Working from the pattern on page 157, cut out from the dark
yellow ribbon 3 sets of A petals, 2 sets of B petals and 3 sets of
C petals; and from the light yellow ribbon, 6 D petals and 10 E
petals. Cut out 1 large and 1 small leaf from the green ribbon.

Roll up 1 set of A petals with the front surface turned outside
and bind the base with wire (#30) and tape (figures 1 and 2).
For the remaining A, B and C petals, twist wire (#30) around
each base (figure 3). Around the rolled A petals, wrap the
remaining 2 sets of A petals with the front surface turned inside
and bind the base with wire (#30) and tape (figure 4). Then
wrap the B petals around this in the same way, and the C petals

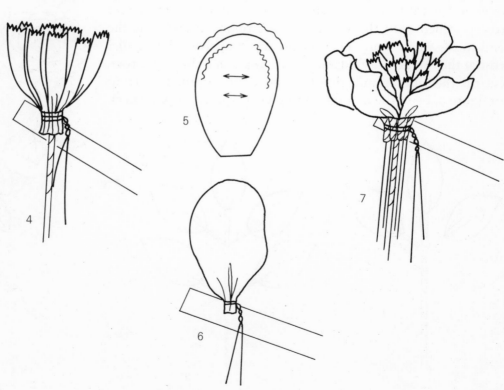

around the A and B petals, fixing the base each time with wire
(#30) and tape.

Stretch the center of each D and E petal sideways and twist
along the edges with your fingertips to create a wavy effect
(figure 5). Then bind the base with wire (#30) and floral tape
(figure 6).

Arrange the D petals around the bound A, B and C petals
with the front surface inside and bind the base with wire (#30)
and tape (figure 7). The E petals are fixed in a similar way
around the D petals with wire (#30). Attach 2 pieces of wire
(#18) to the base of the peony with tape and wind the tape
down the rest of the wire (figure 8).

To make the leaves, bend 3 pieces of wire (#24) in the shape
shown in figure 9 and wind tape from the four-inch join downward. Glue the wires formed in this way to the backs of the
leaves, about 1 in. from the tips, and bind at the base with wire
(#30) and tape (figure 10). About 3 in. below the base of the
flower, attach a small leaf with tape on a leaf stalk about 1 in.
long. Then 4 in. below this, attach the large leaf with wire and
tape (figure 11).

Note: If the ribbon is not wide enough to make the leaf, stick
2 pieces of ribbon 2 in. wide together.

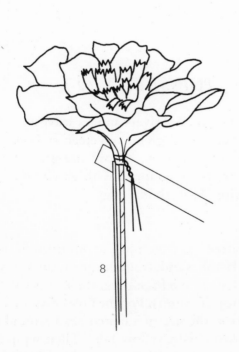

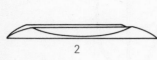

POINSETTIA (1)

MATERIALS (for 1 sprig)
   LEAVES: Red satin ribbon, 3 in. wide
   8 in. of gold glitter ribbon, 1/4 in. wide
   1 piece of wire (#30), 8 in. long

Cut out 3 leaves from the satin ribbon according to the pattern on page 159.

As shown in figure 1, fold each leaf lengthwise in half with the front surface of the ribbon inside. Then fold back the edge of each half outward (figure 2).

Arrange the 3 folded leaves side by side and twist wire (#30) around the middle to hold them together. Then wind tape down the wire (figures 3 and 4). Tie a piece of gold glitter ribbon in the center as shown in figure 5 and spread out the leaves.

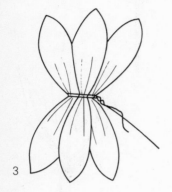

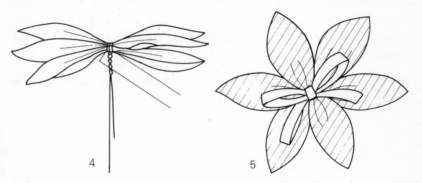

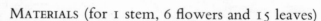

POINSETTIA (2)

MATERIALS (for 1 stem, 6 flowers and 15 leaves)
   LEAVES: Red velvet and green velveteen ribbon, 3 in. wide
   FLOWERS: Absorbent cotton, yellow and green floral tape
   15 pieces of wire (#26) wrapped with green tape, 5 in. long
   10 pieces of wire (#30), 10 in. long
   Glue

Following the pattern on page 159, cut out from the red ribbon 5 A leaves and 5 B leaves and, from the green ribbon, 5 C leaves.

Attach wire (#26) to the back of all the leaves (A, B and C), 1/2 in. from the top (figure 1). For the flower, twirl a small ball of absorbent cotton the size of a match head around the tip of wire (#30) and cover with yellow tape. Then wrap the lower half with light green tape (figures 2 and 3). Make 6 flowers using the same method and bind them all together with wire (#30) and tape (figure 4).

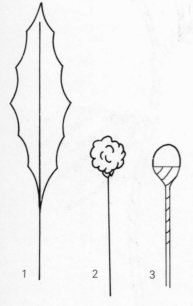

Then, following figure 5, fix the A leaves around the flower with wire (#30) and tape. Under the A leaves, arrange the 5 B leaves in an alternating pattern and fix them on the stem with wire (#30) and tape. Attach the C leaves in the same manner and, after binding the base with wire (#30), wind floral tape down the length of the stem.

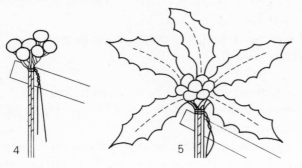

A SILK FLOWER

MATERIALS (for 1 flower)
   1 piece of thin silk, 6–8 in. square
   1 piece of wire (#18)
   1 piece of wire (#30), 8 in. long
   Floral tape the same color as the silk
   Absorbent cotton

Fold 1 corner of the square (figure 1) and roll the strip from the top right-hand corner as shown in figures 2 and 3.

In order to give it a roundish shape, insert a ball of absorbent cotton in the middle of the folded material and bind the base with wire (#30) (figures 4 and 5). Then add the stem wire (#18) with tape, extending it down the entire length of the wire (figure 6).

Note: When arranging a bouquet of silk flowers for display, a more flowing effect may be obtained by using piano wire instead of wire (#18).

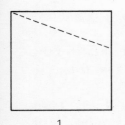

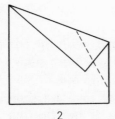

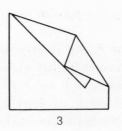

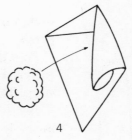

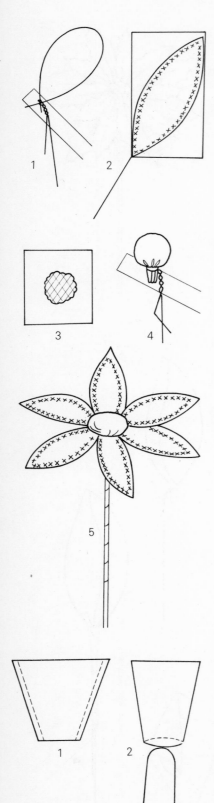

A CHENILLE FLOWER

MATERIALS (for 1 stem and 1 flower)
  Left-over fabric
  6 pieces of chenille, 10 in. long
  5 pieces of wire (#18)
  2 pieces of wire (#30), 8 in. long
  Floral tape (matching the color of the flower)
  Absorbent cotton   Glue

Using the pattern on page 159 as a guide, cut out a strip for the center disk, and 6 rectangular petal strips. Draw the outline of the petal on each strip.

Make a loop with a piece of chenille and bind the two ends together 1/2 in. from the tips with wire (#30) and tape (figure 1). Glue the looped chenille to the front surface of the petal material. Then cut out the petal (figure 2).

For the center disk, make a ball about 1 in. in diameter by wrapping absorbent cotton in a piece of material and twisting wire (#30) and tape around its neck (figures 3 and 4). Arrange 6 petals around the center disk and bind with wire (#30) and tape. Then attach 5 pieces of wire (#18) to the base with tape and wind it down the whole length of the stem (figure 5).

A POLKA DOT FLOWER

MATERIALS (for 2 flowers)
  Polka dot fabric
  2 buttons
  2 pieces of wire (#18)
  6 pieces of wire (#20), 12 in. long
  Floral tape to match the color of the flower
  Cotton thread   Glue

Following the pattern on page 160, cut out 3 A, 3 B and 6 C petals.

Fold the A and B strips in half, with the front surface of the material inside (figure 1), and sew both sides 1/2 in. from the edge. Then turn it over, right side out.

Bend a piece of wire (#20) in a horseshoe shape. Then insert it through the opening at the bottom, bending it at various places to fit the inside of the sewn material (figure 2).

Twist wire (#30) around the base and wind tape over it (figure 3). Glue petal C on top of each A and B petal, as seen in figure 4.

Insert wire (#30) through the hole underneath the button and twist it at the neck. Then wind tape over the wire (figure 5). Fix 3 A petals around the button with wire (#30), attach the stem wire (#18) and cover it with tape (figures 6 and 7). The same procedure is used for the B petals.

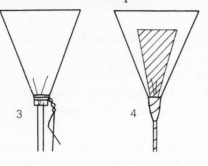

A STITCHED FLOWER

MATERIALS (for 2 flowers)
   Thick unfrayable fabric
   10 pieces of wire (#18)
   2 pieces of wire (#30), 8 in. long
   Thick silk thread
   Floral tape to match the color of the flower

Following the pattern on page 160, cut out 4 A petals and 4 B petals.

Stitch the A petals together at a point about two-thirds from the bottom, using a matching silk thread (figure 1). Be sure to have the seam on the front surface of the material (figure 2).

Put 4 pieces of wire (#18) together, leave 1 1/2 in. of the tip bare and wind tape about 3 in. down it (figure 3). As shown in figure 4, pass the wires through the flower and spread them out, binding the base of the flower with wire (#30). Then add another piece of wire (#18) for the stem and wind tape down the entire stem.

Repeat the same procedure to make the flower using the B petals.

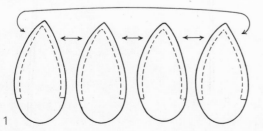

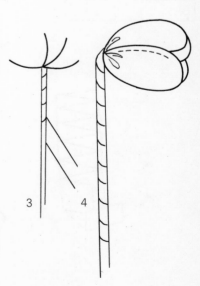

A FOLDED PAPER FLOWER

MATERIALS (for 1 flower)
  FLOWER: Beige, dark brown or moss green thick paper
  3 pieces of wire (#22), 8 in. long
  1 piece of wire (#18)
  Yellow floral tape

Cut the paper into a long narrow strip, 1 1/4 in. × 32 in. in size. Fold it in half and, at the center of the strip, fold it as shown in figure 1. Then fold the lower end (A) upward and the upper end (B) sideways to the left (figure 2). Continue folding A and B alternately (figures 3 and 4). The final end is tucked into the previous fold (figure 5).

Take both ends and staple them together to make a circle (figures 6 and 7). Wind tape round 3 pieces of wire (#22) separately. Then put the 3 pieces together and bind them with tape down to the end, beginning about 3 1/2 in. from the top (figure 8). Working from figure 9, pass the wire through the center of the flower and spread out the tips. Attach wire (#18) to the base of the flower with tape and wind the tape down its whole length.

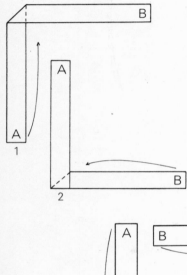

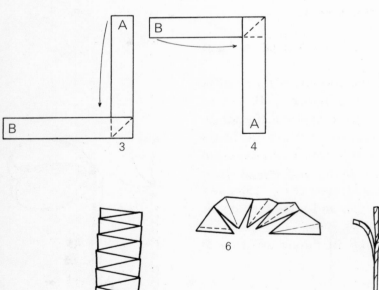

PATTERNS

TULIP

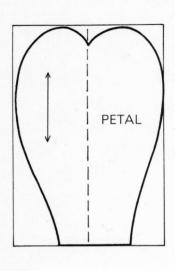

PETAL

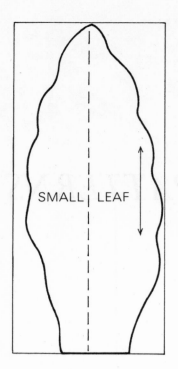

SMALL LEAF

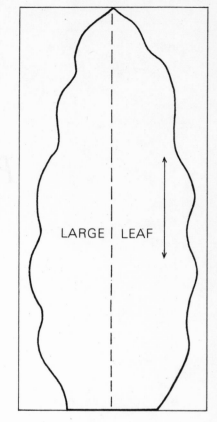

LARGE LEAF

MARGUERITE

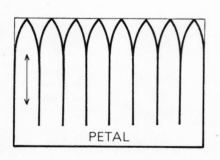

PETAL

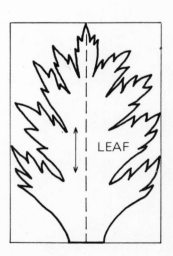

LEAF

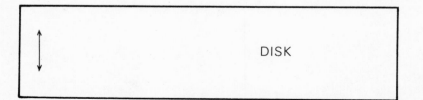

DISK

MINIATURE ROSE

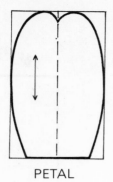

PETAL

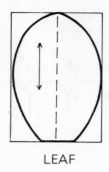

LEAF

WOOD ROSE

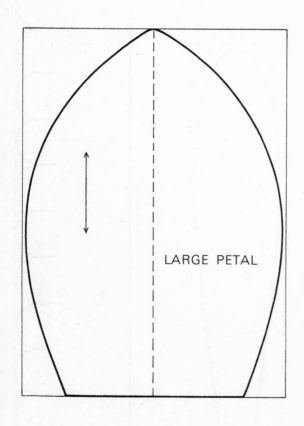

LARGE PETAL

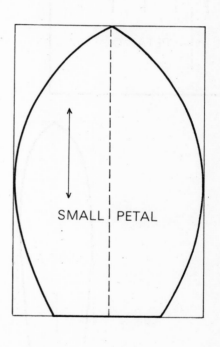

SMALL PETAL

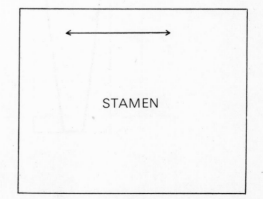

STAMEN

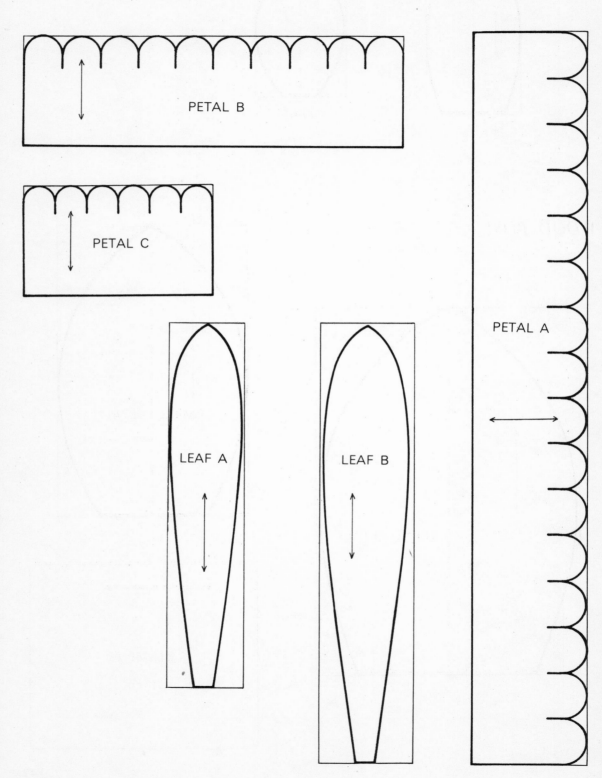

PETAL B

PETAL C

LEAF A

LEAF B

PETAL A

HIBISCUS

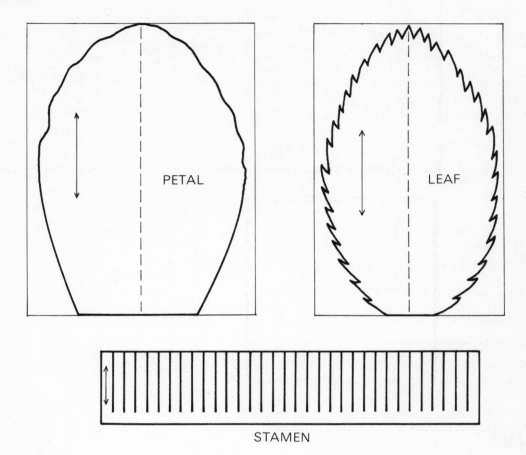

PETAL

LEAF

STAMEN

COSMOS

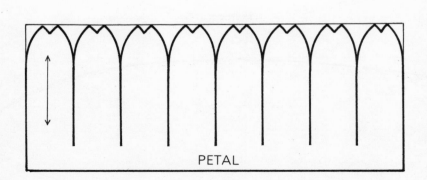

PETAL

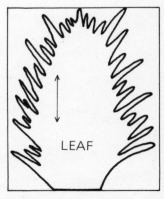

LEAF

(continued overleaf)

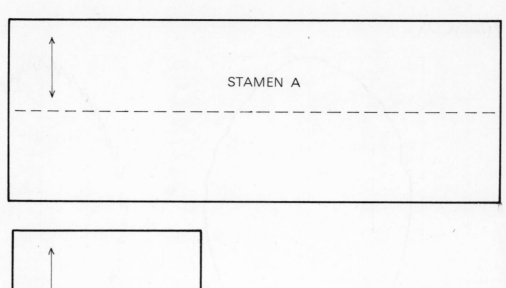

STAMEN A

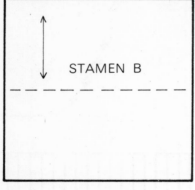

STAMEN B

LILY

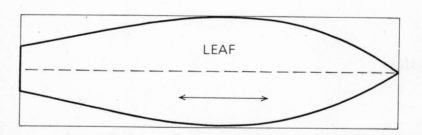

LEAF

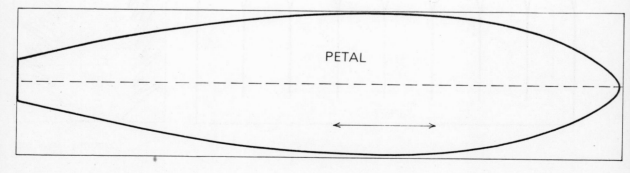

PETAL

HYDRANGEA

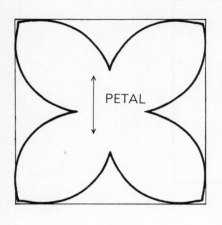

PETAL

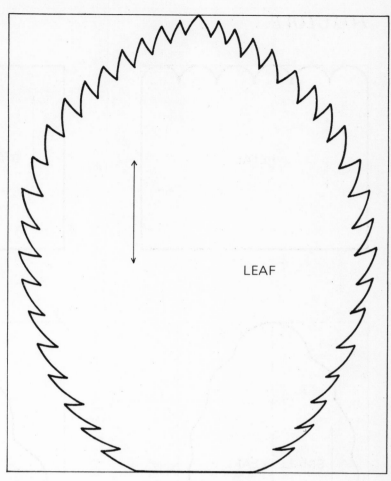

LEAF

SNAPDRAGON

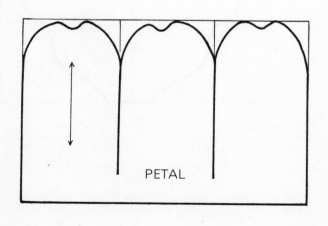

PETAL

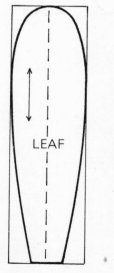

LEAF

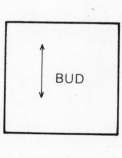

BUD

FOXGLOVE

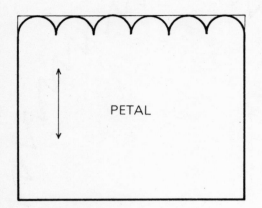

PETAL

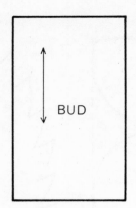

BUD

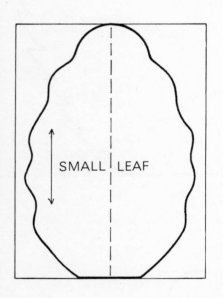

SMALL LEAF

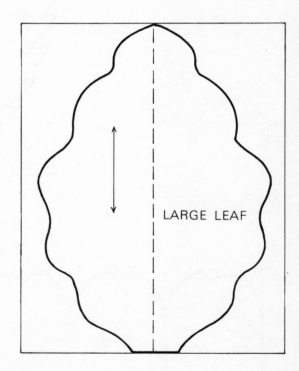

LARGE LEAF

GLADIOLUS

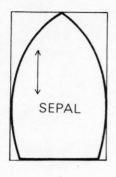

SEPAL

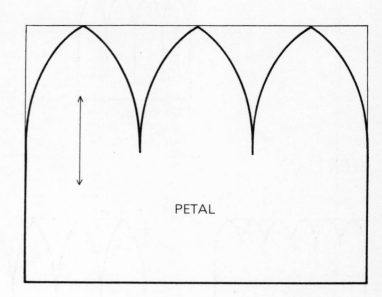

PETAL

10 in. (large leaf), 8 in. (small leaf)

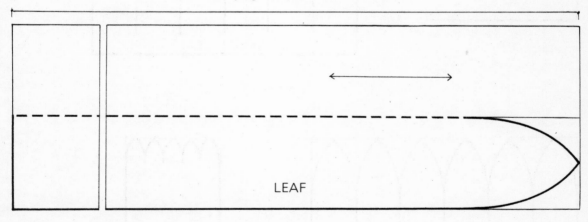

LEAF

FORSYTHIA

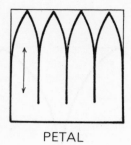

PETAL

GENTIAN

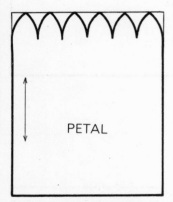

PETAL

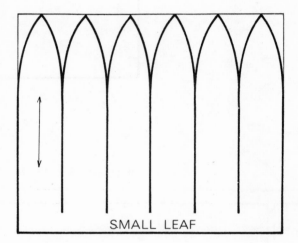

SMALL LEAF

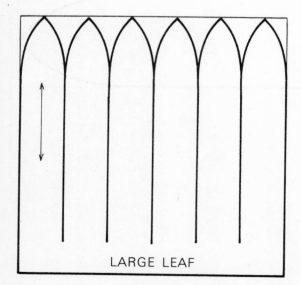

LARGE LEAF

CALYX

DAISY

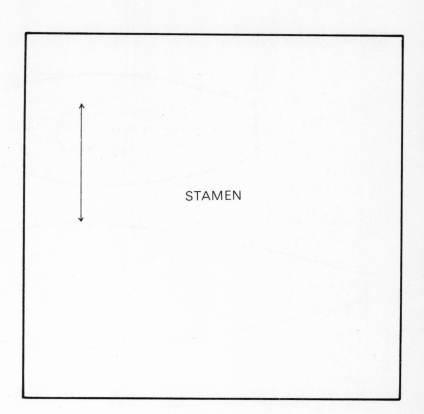

STAMEN

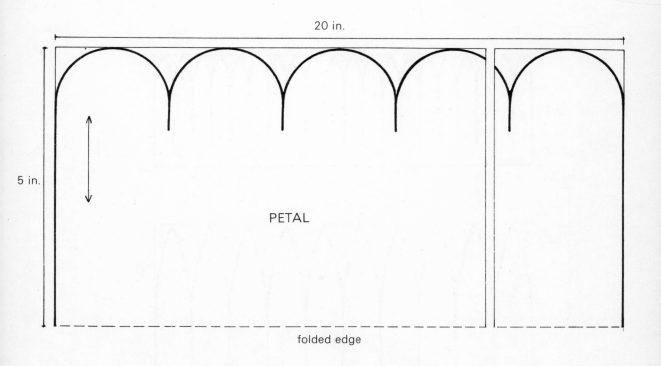

20 in.

5 in.

PETAL

folded edge

RHODODENDRON

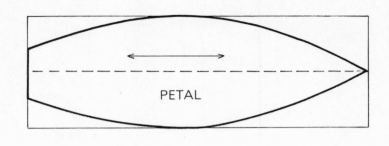

PETAL

LEAF

EDELWEISS

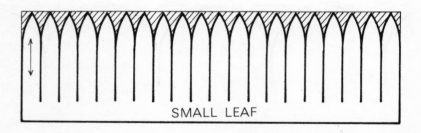

SMALL LEAF

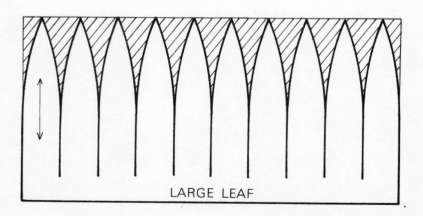

LARGE LEAF

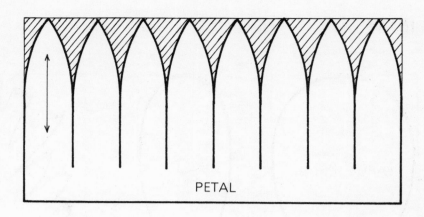

PETAL

BOUVARDIA

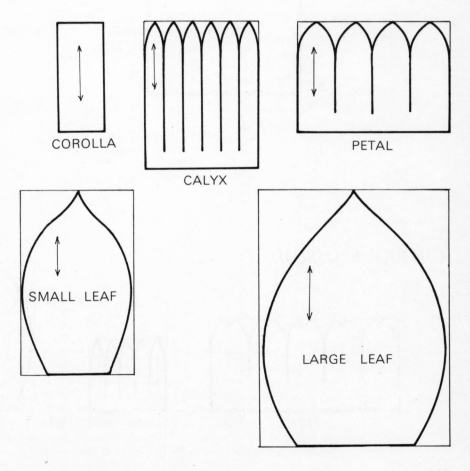

COROLLA

CALYX

PETAL

SMALL LEAF

LARGE LEAF

ANEMONE

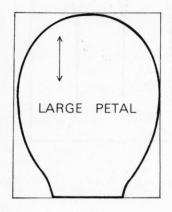

LARGE PETAL

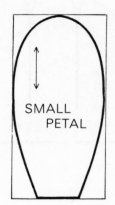

SMALL PETAL

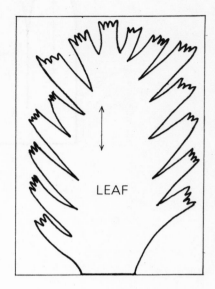

LEAF

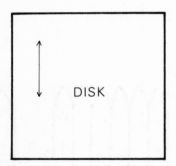

DISK

CHERRY BLOSSOM

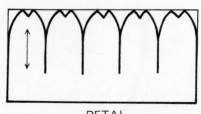

PETAL

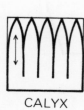

CALYX

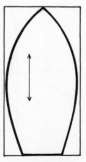

LEAF

GARDENIA

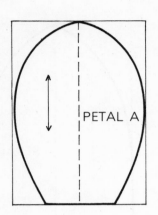

PETAL A

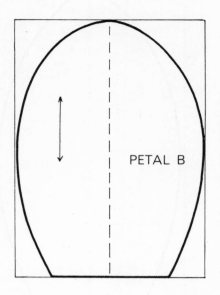

PETAL B

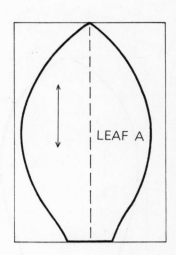

LEAF A

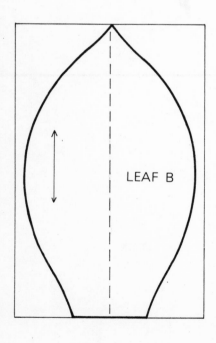

LEAF B

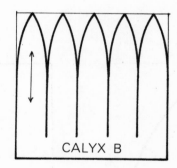

CALYX B

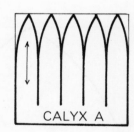

CALYX A

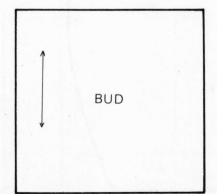

BUD

POMPON DAHLIA

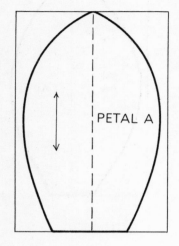

PETAL A

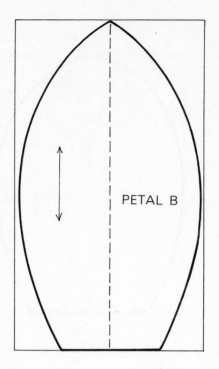

PETAL B

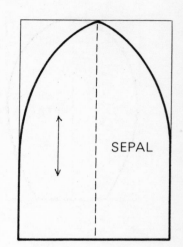

SEPAL

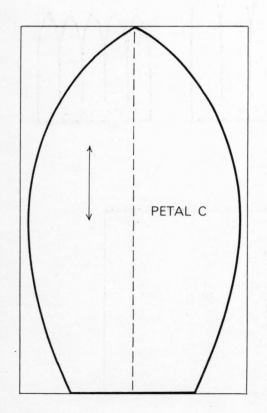

PETAL C

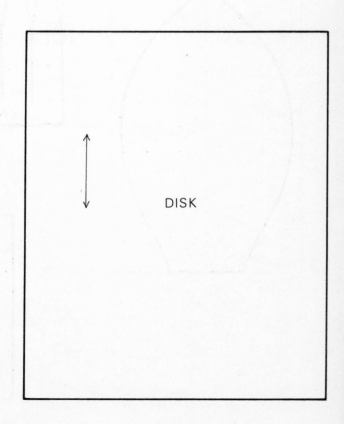

DISK

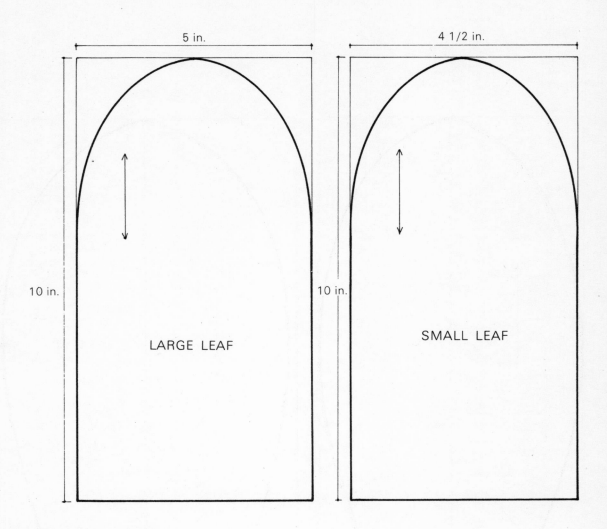

5 in.

4 1/2 in.

10 in.

LARGE LEAF

10 in.

SMALL LEAF

CACTUS DAHLIA

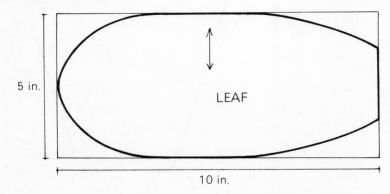

5 in.

LEAF

10 in.

(continued overleaf)

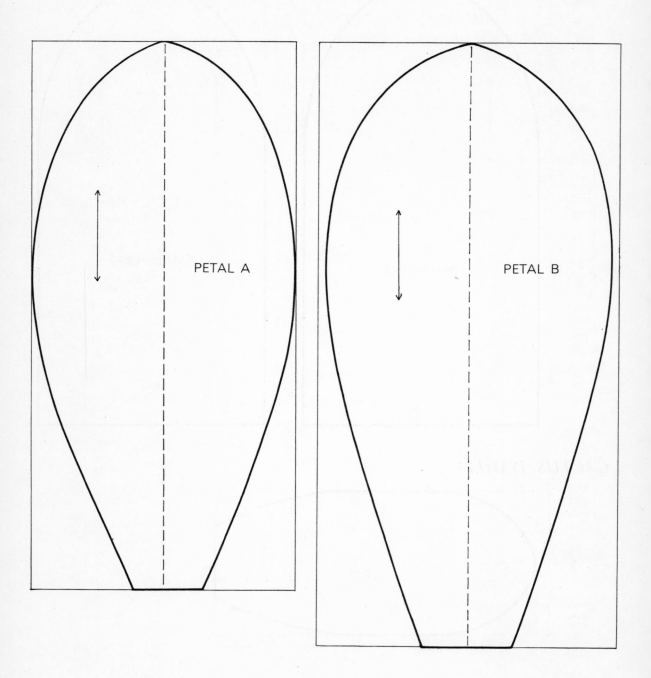

PETAL A

PETAL B

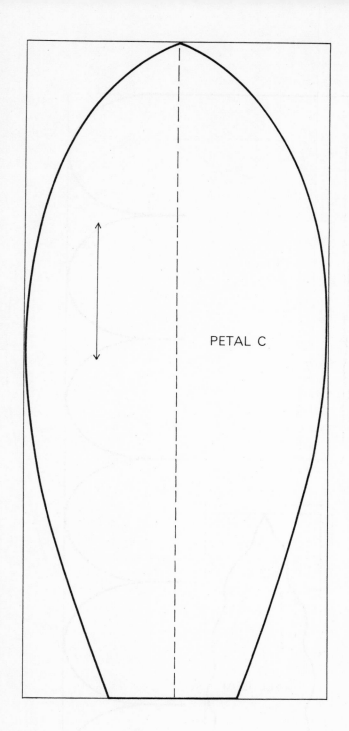

PETAL C

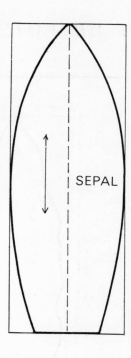

SEPAL

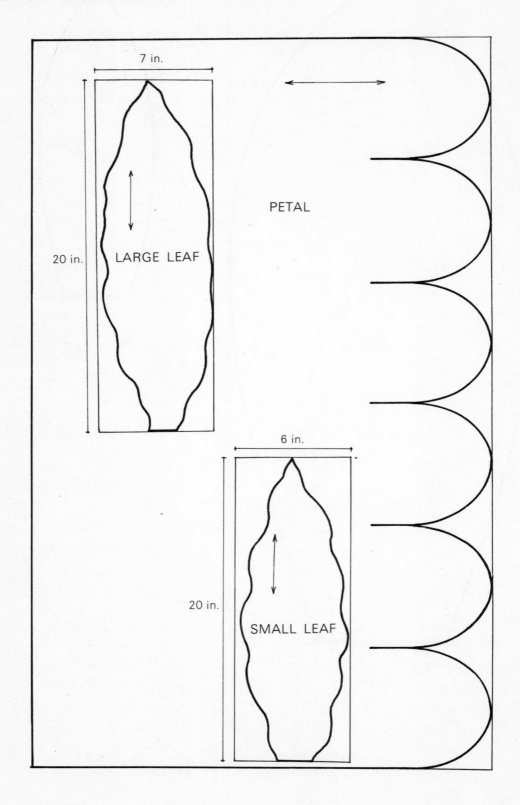

7 in.

20 in.

LARGE LEAF

PETAL

6 in.

20 in.

SMALL LEAF

POPPY

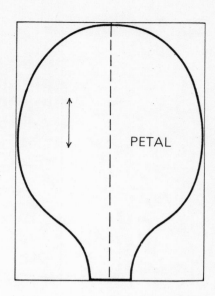

PETAL

STEM

HYACINTH

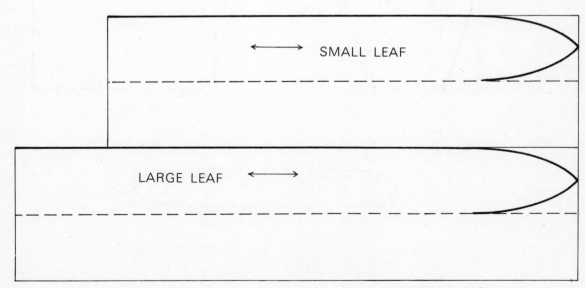

SMALL LEAF

LARGE LEAF

(continued overleaf)

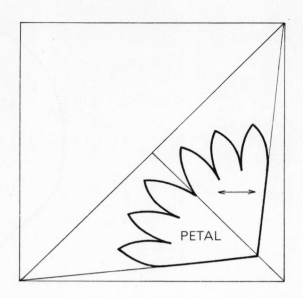

PETAL

CARNATION

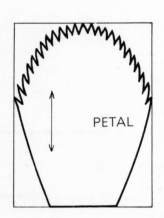

PETAL

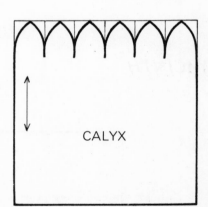

CALYX

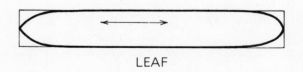

LEAF

DAFFODIL

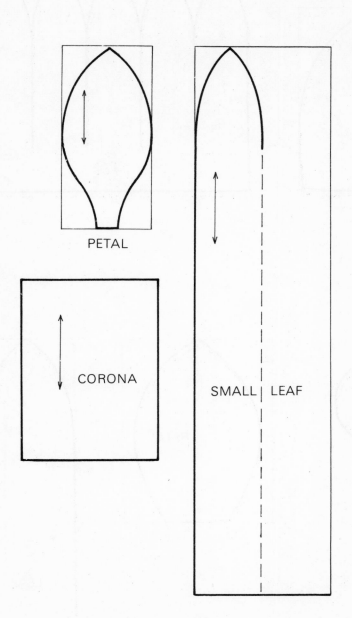

PETAL

CORONA

SMALL | LEAF

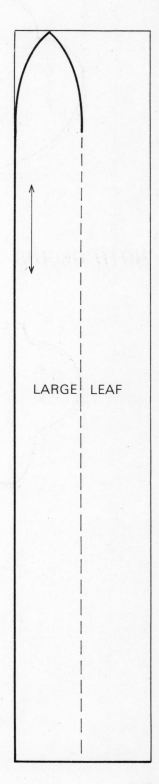

LARGE | LEAF

EVENING PRIMROSE

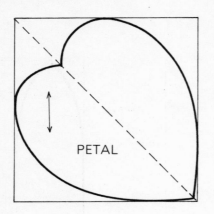

PETAL

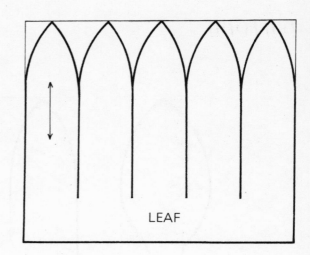

LEAF

MOTH ORCHID

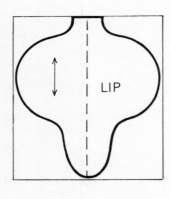

LIP

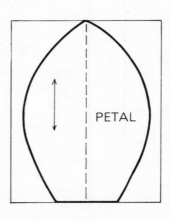

PETAL

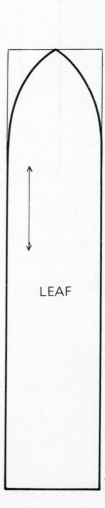

LEAF

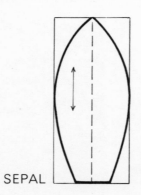

SEPAL

ROSE

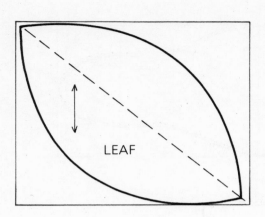

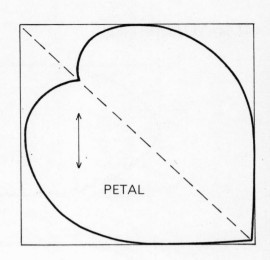

LEAF

PETAL

OLD WORLD ORCHID

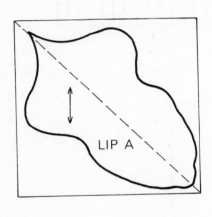

LIP A

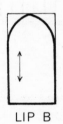

LIP B

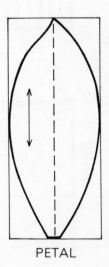

PETAL

20 in. (large leaf), 16 in. (medium leaf), 8 in. (small leaf)

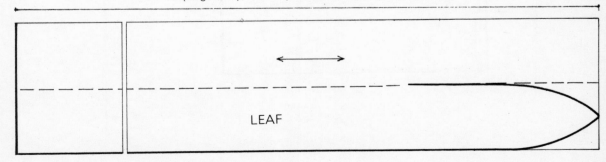

LEAF

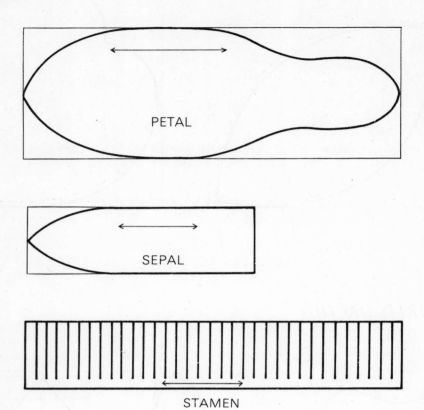

PETAL

SEPAL

STAMEN

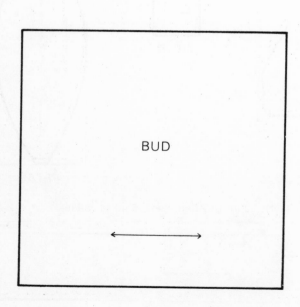

BUD

A EUCALYPTUS FANTASY

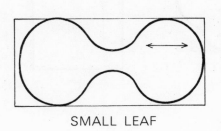

SMALL LEAF

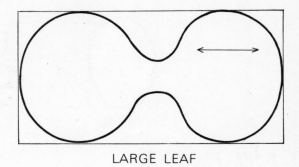

LARGE LEAF

CAMELLIA

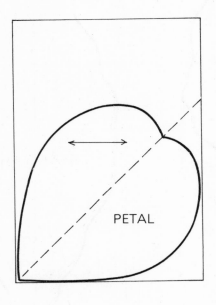

PETAL

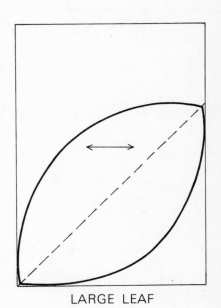

LARGE LEAF

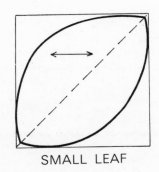

SMALL LEAF

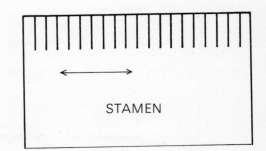

STAMEN

PEACH BLOSSOM

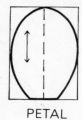

PETAL

CALYX

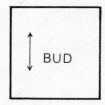

BUD

RAPE FLOWER

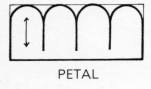

PETAL

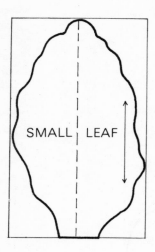

SMALL LEAF

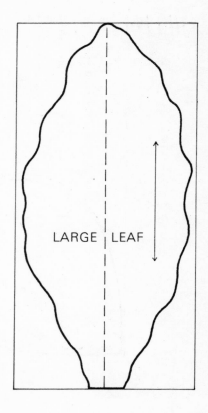

LARGE LEAF

IRIS

20 in. (large leaf), 16 in. (small leaf)

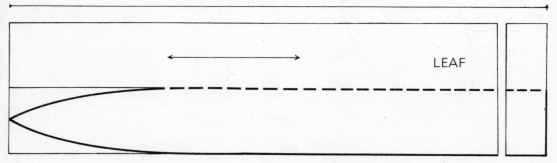

LEAF

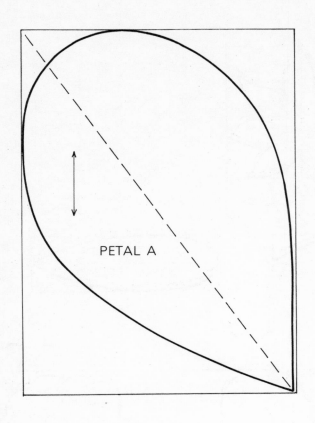

PETAL A

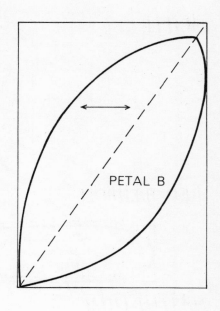

PETAL B

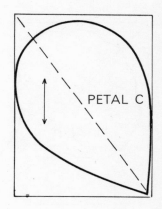

PETAL C

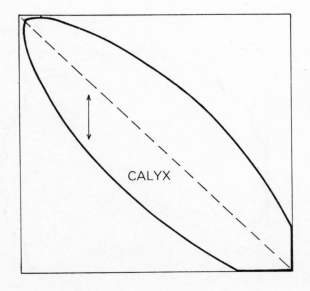

CALYX

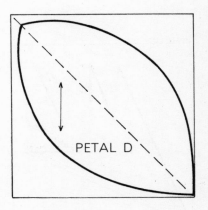

PETAL D

MAPLE

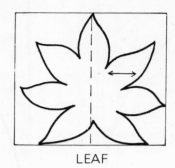

LEAF

RED BAMBOO

LARGE LEAF

SMALL LEAF

NASTURTIUM

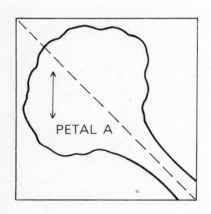

PETAL A

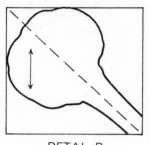

PETAL B

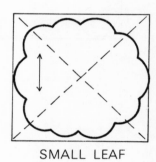

SMALL LEAF

CALYX

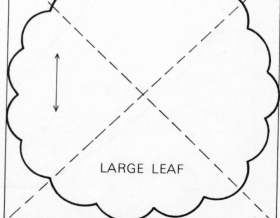

LARGE LEAF

FLOWERET

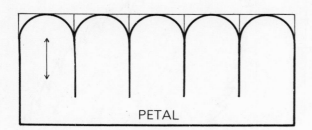

PETAL

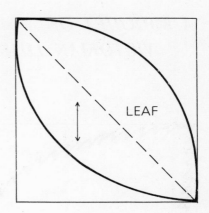

LEAF

CATTLEYA

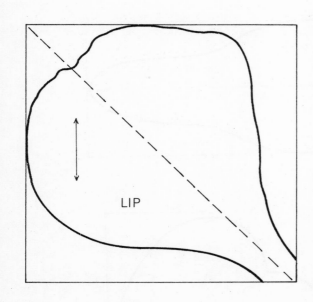

LIP

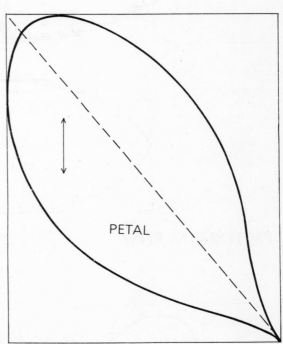

PETAL

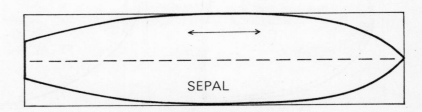

SEPAL

A BOUQUET OF
VICTORIAN LILIES

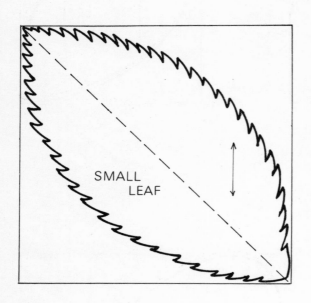

SMALL
LEAF

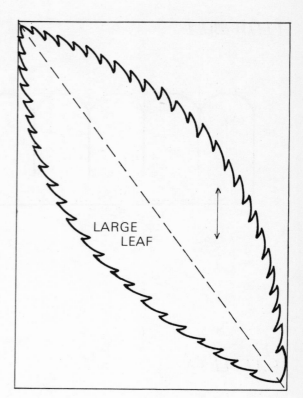

LARGE
LEAF

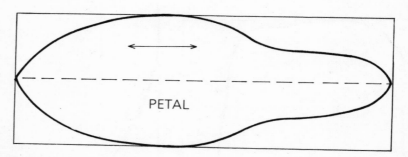

PETAL

VICTORIAN ROSE

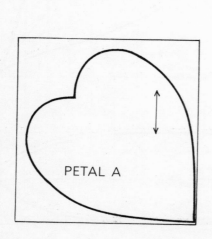

PETAL A

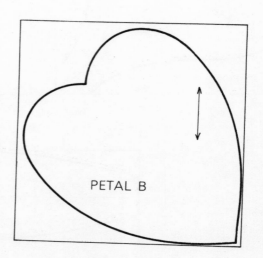

PETAL B

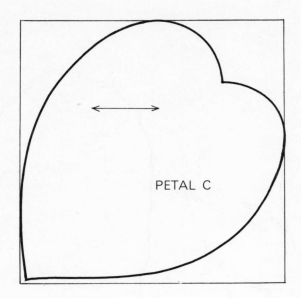

PETAL C

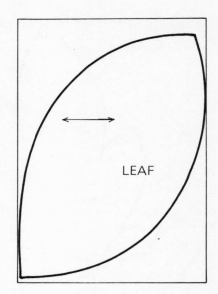

LEAF

PEONY

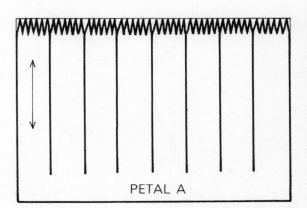

PETAL A

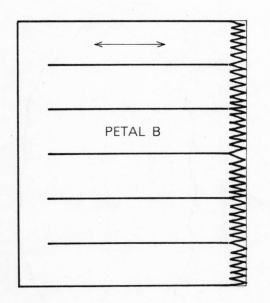

PETAL B

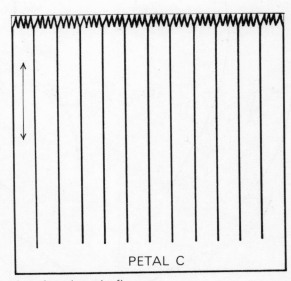

PETAL C

(continued overleaf)

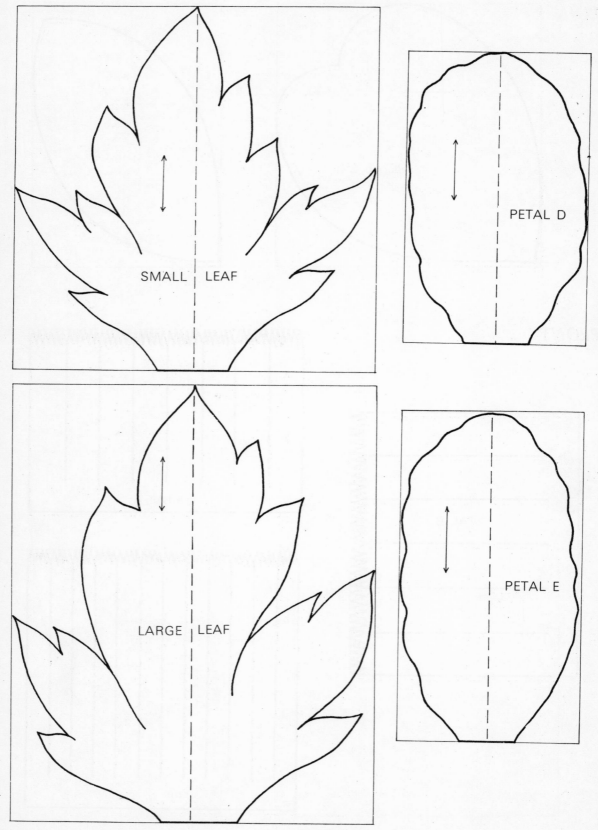

SMALL LEAF

PETAL D

LARGE LEAF

PETAL E

158

POINSETTIA (1)

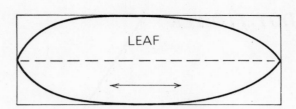

LEAF

POINSETTIA (2)

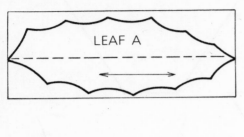

LEAF A

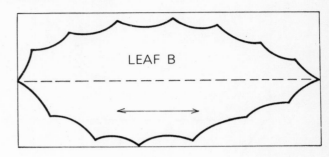

LEAF B

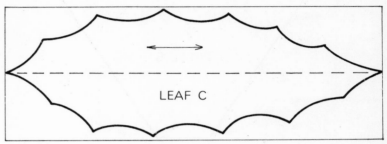

LEAF C

A CHENILLE FLOWER

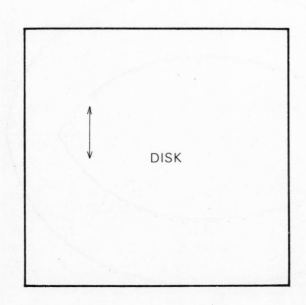

DISK

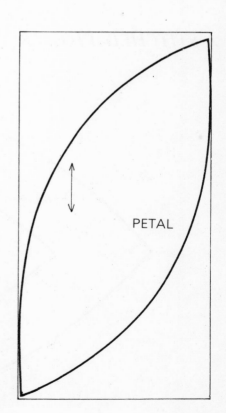

PETAL

A POLKA DOT FLOWER

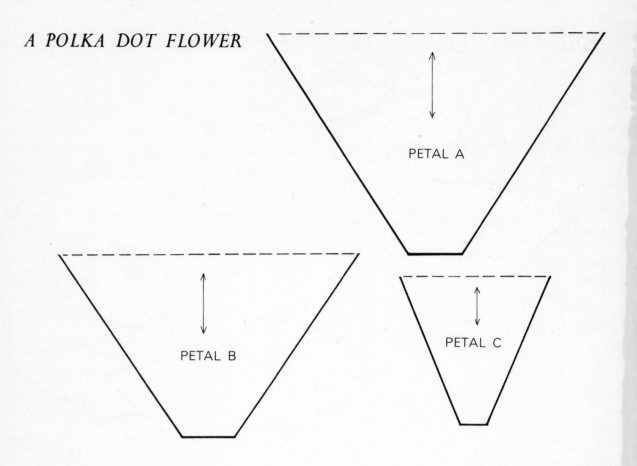

PETAL A

PETAL B

PETAL C

A STITCHED FLOWER

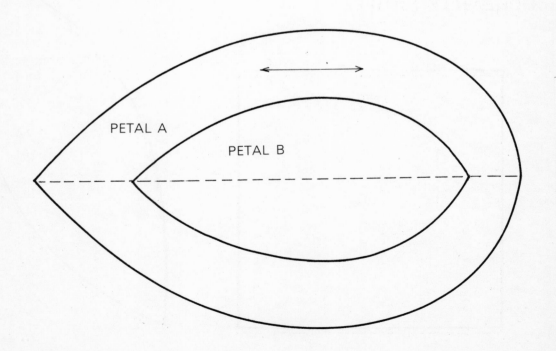

PETAL A

PETAL B